standards

FOR EDUCATIONAL & PSYCHOLOGICAL TESTS

Prepared by a joint committee of the
American Psychological Association
American Educational Research Association
National Council on Measurement in Education
Frederick B. Davis, *Chair*

Published by the
AMERICAN   PSYCHOLOGICAL   ASSOCIATION,   INC.
1200 Seventeenth Street, N.W.   •   Washington, D.C. 20036

This book is a revision of the 1966 Standards for *Educational and Psychological Tests and Manuals,* published by the American Psychological Association.

Published by the American Psychological Association, Inc.
1200 Seventeenth Street, N.W., Washington, D.C. 20036

Office of Scientific Affairs
Miriam F. Kelty, *Administrative Officer*
Willo P. White, *Administrative Associate*

Office of Communications
Harold P. Van Cott, *Director*
Elliot R. Siegel, *Executive Editor for Separate Publications*
Pamela A. Taylor, *Editor*
Elizabeth V. Forrester, *Editor*

Printed in the United States of America

FOREWORD

This document is the lineal descendant of *Technical Recommendations for Psychological Tests and Diagnostic Techniques,* prepared by a committee of the American Psychological Association and published by that organization in 1954, and of *Technical Recommendations for Achievement Tests,* prepared by committees of the American Educational Research Association and the National Council on Measurements Used in Education and published by the National Education Association in 1955. In 1966, the American Psychological Association, the American Educational Research Association, and the National Council on Measurement in Education published *Standards for Educational and Psychological Tests and Manuals* (through the American Psychological Association) to replace the two earlier documents.

By 1971, it had become apparent that problems and issues in testing, especially problems in selection for employment or for admission to educational institutions, had outdated the 1966 publication. Consequently, the Committee on Psychological Tests of the American Psychological Association (later merged with the Committee on Assessment) made contact with the American Educational Research Association and the National Council on Measurement in Education to form a joint committee for the revision of *Standards for Educational and Psychological Tests and Manuals.* The members of the joint committee were:

Philip Ash (APA)
Joan K. Bollenbacher (NCME)
Frederick B. Davis, Chairman (APA)
Robert L. Ebel (APA)
Edmund W. Gordon (APA)
Robert M. Guion (APA)

George F. Madaus (NCME)
William A. Mehrens (AERA)
Doris P. Mosby (APA)
James H. Ricks (AERA)
E. Belvin Williams (liaison with the APA Board of Scientific Affairs)

The principal author of *Standards for Educational and Psychological Tests* is Professor Robert M. Guion, Bowling Green State University, Bowling Green, Ohio. The committee expresses to him and to dozens of other psychologists and educators who provided comments and suggestions with respect to early drafts of the document its deep appreciation for their contributions. Special gratitude is owing to the following who generously read and commented on the final draft: Anne Anastasi, Nancy Cole, Lee J. Cronbach, Robert L. Linn, Julian C. Stanley, and Robert L. Thorndike. The joint committee is deeply indebted to Miriam F. Kelty and Willo P. White of the Central Office of the American Psychological Association for their assistance throughout the project.

Because some members of the joint committee judged that certain aspects of program evaluation and of the interpretation of scores derived from content-referenced tests have not been treated adequately within the scope of the present document, the committee has suggested that publication of a companion volume be considered by a succeeding joint committee.

Finally, the chairman of the committee wishes to express to members of the present committee his deep appreciation of their long hours of critical reading and committee discussion.

Frederick B. Davis
University of Pennsylvania

INTRODUCTION

In March, 1954, the American Psychological Association issued the *Technical Recommendations for Psychological Tests and Diagnostic Techniques*, endorsed by the American Educational Research Association and the National Council on Measurement in Education. In January, 1955, the latter two organizations published a further document, *Technical Recommendations for Achievement Tests*. Subsequently, a joint committee of the three organizations consolidated, modified, and revised the two documents and in 1966, through the American Psychological Association, published the *Standards for Educational and Psychological Tests and Manuals*. The present document is both a revision and an extension of the 1966 *Standards*. It presents standards for test use as well as for test manuals; it is intended to guide both test developers and test users.

A test user is one who chooses tests, interprets scores, or makes decisions based on test scores. (People who do only routine administration or scoring of tests are not included in this definition, although test users often do both.) Test users include clinical or industrial psychologists, research directors, school psychologists, counselors, employment supervisors, teachers, and various administrators who select or interpret tests for their organizations. The audience for the *Standards* is, therefore, broad and cuts across publics with varying backgrounds and different training in measurement and statistics. Sections of the *Standards*, particularly those related to validity and reliability, are necessarily technical. These two sections should be meaningful to readers who have training approximately equivalent to a level between the master's degree and the doctorate in education or psychology. However, the remaining sections—the greater part of the document—are generally nontechnical and may be read with profit by all users.

The authors of the 1966 *Standards* declared that a test producer has an obligation to provide enough information about a test so that a qualified user will know what reliance can safely be placed on it; they also provided statements of consensus concerning the information that should be in a manual. It now appears desirable to provide similar statements of consensus concerning competency in testing practices.

Part of the stimulus for revision is an awakened concern about problems like invasion of privacy or discrimination against members of groups such as minorities or women. Serious misuses of tests include, for example, labeling Spanish-speaking children as mentally retarded on the basis of scores on tests standardized on "a representative sample of American children," or using a test with a major loading on verbal comprehension without appropriate validation in an attempt to screen out large numbers of blacks from manipulative jobs requiring minimal verbal communication.

These are specific examples of a general problem of test appropriateness. A test score describes but it does not explain a level of performance. Test performance may be influenced by many factors such as amount and quality of certain kinds of training, distractions during testing, sensory defects, inability to hear instructions because of poor administration, inappropriate language in instructions or in the test, inability to read, brain damage, motivation level, illumination level, cultural background of the examinee, or test-taking strategies.

Some unfairness may be built into a test, for example, requiring an inordinately high level of verbal ability to comprehend the instructions for a nonverbal test. Many of the social ills attributed to tests, however, seem more a result of the ways in which tests have been used than of characteristics of the tests themselves; for example, errors in administration, failure to consider the appropriateness of normative data, failure to choose an appropriate test, use of incorrect assumptions about the causes of a low or deviant test score, or administrative rigidity in using test scores for making decisions.

Tests and Test Uses to Which These Standards Apply

It is intended that these standards apply to any assessment procedure, assessment device, or assessment aid; that is, to any systematic basis for making inferences about characteristics of people.

A test is a special case of an assessment procedure. It may be thought of as a set of tasks or questions intended to elicit particular types of

behavior when presented under standardized conditions and to yield scores that will have desirable psychometric properties such as high reliability and high validity.

Tests include standardized aptitude and achievement instruments, diagnostic and evaluative devices, interest inventories, personality inventories, projective instruments and related clinical techniques, and many kinds of personal history forms. It was pointed out in the 1966 *Standards* that the same general types of information are needed for all these varieties of published diagnostic, prognostic, and evaluative devices. It is equally appropriate to point out that unpublished assessment devices can be better used if the same kind of information is available to users.[1]

---

[1] It is sometimes suggested in response to perceptions of test abuse and unfair uses of tests that a moratorium on testing be observed until better and more appropriate instruments are developed and more equitable procedures can be instituted. The suggestion of such an extreme measure may be indicative of the growing sense of frustration and indignation felt particularly by some minority group members who sense that testing has had a disproportionately negative impact on their opportunities for equal access to success in education and employment. This suggestion, although well intended, seems futile for several reasons:

First, it fails to consider unfairness resulting from the misuses of tests. If new and better tests were subject to the same sorts of misuse, they might well produce the same sorts of errors (or errors of the same magnitudes) in the decisions based on them.

Second, it requires a corresponding but unlikely moratorium on decisions. Employers will continue to make employment decisions with or without standardized tests. Colleges and universities will still select students, some elementary pupils will still be recommended for special education, and boards of education will continue to evaluate the success of specific programs. If

There are wide variations in the sophistication of assessment techniques. At one extreme is the test that has gone through several revisions based on many research studies. Such a test may provide normative data based on thousands of cases classified into dozens of subpopulations. At the other extreme is the casual interview that provides assessments based on varying and unsystematically observed cues.

These standards are written specifically to apply to standardized tests. They apply in varying degrees, however, to the entire range of assessment techniques. If it is required that a relationship be demonstrated between scores (assessments) on an employment test and subsequent performance on a job, the requirement should in principle also apply to the judgments (assessments) of the employment interviewer. It may not be possible to apply the standards with the same rigor, but the kind of judgments the interviewer is to make can be identified; the time and procedures for developing and recording them can be standardized; and they can be validated in the same ways that scores are validated. When someone who makes personnel decisions develops his own assessment techniques (a practice not discouraged intentionally in these stan-

dards), he will find the standards useful guides for developing information similar to that in good test manuals; the principles are as relevant to him as to the professional test developer. If he chooses to use a test that has been developed by someone else, he may find the standards helpful in evaluating alternatives from which he may choose; moreover, the standards may help in developing a program of application.

There are many dimensions along which measuring instruments can be classified. Some are designed to measure abilities, some to measure accomplishments, others to measure attitudes or interests. Some are inventories, interview aids, biographical data forms, and experimental diagnostic devices, and are not called tests. Generally, however, the word "test" is used in these standards to apply to all kinds of measurement. What these different kinds have in common is that scores with desirable psychometric properties may be derived from each.

These standards also apply to *criterion measures.* Studies evaluating uses of well-developed tests too often employ inadequate criterion data. A criterion measure should have the psychometric properties expected of any other measurement, such as validity, including in special instances some form of criterion-related validity, for example, the relationship of an immediate criterion measure to an intermediate or more nearly ultimate measure. Criterion development should be guided by the standards guiding test development.

Some assessment techniques are used as interview aids. The intent of such use

---

those responsible for making decisions do not use standardized assessment techniques, they will use less dependable methods of assessment.

Third, tests are often useful for *finding* talent but are too often used only as devices for rejecting those with low scores; they can also be used to discover potential for performance that might not otherwise be observed. In this way, the use of tests may sometimes improve the prospects of minority group members and women.

is an idiographic analysis of an individual—an approach to assessment which places special reliance on the skill of the clinician. It is often argued that this use is so unlike the use of other testing procedures that it cannot be judged by essentially psychometric standards. The qualitative nature of the assessment is less the point at issue than the distinction that can be made between clinical and actuarial prediction. When tests, projective or otherwise, are used as aids to an interviewer's assessment, the interviewer is himself the final assessment device, and his assessments become the "scores." These assessments can and should be validated like other psychometric measures.

Component bits of information may be analyzed somewhat as items are analyzed. Proposals for arriving at idiographic interpretations are almost always based partially upon a nomothetic premise; for example, that a Rorschach determinant correlates with a specified internal factor. The usual standards can be applied to premises of this kind. Therefore, although interview aids can present unusual problems, their user requires the same information about them that he requires for any test score, and his use of them is subject to some of the same psychometric considerations (e.g., reliability) applicable to other test scores.

The developer of such an interview aid need not indicate his test's validity by correlating it with any simple criterion. But if he goes so far as to make any generalization about what "most people see" or what "schizophrenics rarely do," he is making a statistical claim and should be held to the usual rules for supporting it. Moreover, when on the basis of projective test data, biographical information, or various behavioral cues elicited during an interview the interviewer makes a statement such as "this man will fail or be subject to severe depression if placed in this situation," he is making a prediction based on his assessment and should be held to the standards for demonstrating the validity of his prediction.

A comment also seems appropriate about hidden tests (such as an interviewer's systematic attempt to assess a trait within the context of the interview) or other unobtrusive or observational measures. Some of these may raise ethical problems, but they do not differ, in principle, from other tests, and the standards apply as much to these unseen or unrecognized tests as to those more clearly perceived by the examinee. Therefore, the psychologist who counts examples of a specific type of response in a behavior-modification setting is as much responsible for the validity of his interpretations of change or the basic reliability of his observations as is any other test user.

In short, the standards are intended to be widely applicable both to standardized tests and a wide variety of other assessment techniques. The degree of applicability of individual standards to nontest assessments will vary; developers and users of such assessment procedures should at least observe the spirit of the standards.

Tests are used for basic research purposes as well as for practical purposes. Although these standards were not written with research purposes in mind, the qualified investigator should be able to determine the manner in which they apply to his research.

These standards cannot replace instructional material on test development; therefore, there are no specific statements directly related to such procedures as item writing or item analysis.

Information Standards as a Guide to Test Developers

For each test there should be a test manual, perhaps with supplements, to provide enough information for a qualified user to make sound judgments regarding the usefulness and interpretation of test scores. Research is required prior to the release of the test or test scores for operational use.

A manual is to be judged not merely by its literal truthfulness, but by the impression it leaves with the reader. If the typical professional user for whom the manual is prepared is likely to obtain an inaccurate impression of the test from the manual, the manual is poorly written. The standards apply to the spirit and tone of the manual (or supplemental publication) as well as to its literal statements.

A manual must often communicate information to many different groups. Many tests are used by people with limited training in testing. These users may not follow technical discussion or understand detailed statistical information. Other users are measurement specialists; they seek information on which to judge the technical adequacy of the test. Sometimes technical information can be presented in a supplementary handbook. Whatever the form, the prospective test user must have available to him the information needed for making whatever judgments his use of the test requires. Even when the test (or test battery) is developed for use within a single organization, a manual can often be helpful; preparation of a manual helps the test developer organize his thinking, codify his procedures, and communicate his ideas and intentions to his assistants.

It is not appropriate for this publication to call for a particular level of validity or reliability, or otherwise to establish technical test specifications for specific tests, but it is appropriate to ask that any test manual provide the information necessary for a test user to decide whether the consistency, relevance, or standardization of a test makes it suitable for his purpose. These standards need not prescribe minimum statistical specifications. Rather, their intent is to describe in an explicit and conveniently available form the information required by test users. In arriving at those requirements, it has been necessary to judge what is a reasonable compromise between pressures of cost and time, on the one hand, and the ideal, on the other. The test producer ordinarily spends large sums of money in developing and standardizing a test. Insofar as these recommendations indicate the kind of information that is most valuable to test users, authors and publishers can more efficiently allocate funds for gathering and reporting data of greatest value. Some provisions are more applicable than others in any specific case. The completion of predictive validity studies related to job criteria, for example, is essential before a vocational interest inventory can be used properly, but it may be only desirable for a values inventory and irrelevant for an inventory designed to diagnose mental disorders. These standards, therefore, represent an attempt to state what type of studies should be completed before a test is ready for release to the profession. They can serve as a similar guide for those who are developing tests for their own use.

Procedural Standards as a Guide to Test Users

The test user, in selecting, administering, scoring, or interpreting a test, should know his purposes, what he is doing to achieve those purposes, and their probable consequences. It is not enough to have benign purposes; the user must know the procedures necessary to maximize effectiveness and to minimize unfairness in test use. He must evaluate the many factors that may have influenced test performance in light of his purposes. Where he finds that certain factors would unfairly influence performance, his procedures for using the test and interpreting the scores should be designed to minimize such influences.

Competence in test use is a combination of knowledge of psychometric principles, knowledge of the problem situation in which the testing is to be done, technical skill, and some wisdom. Although it is not appropriate to tell a test user that he needs particular levels of validity and reliability, it is appropriate to ask him to ascertain that his procedures result in reasonably valid predictions or reliable clas-

sifications, or otherwise conform to the purposes of his testing. These standards of practice are written more as guidelines than as commandments. It is as necessary to make cost-benefit compromises in test use as in test development. These standards provide useful guidelines for test users as well as for test developers.

Three Levels of Standards

Manuals can never give all the information, and test users can never follow all the procedures that might be desirable. At the same time, restricting this statement of recommendations solely to essential or indispensable information and practices might tend to discourage development and reporting of additional information. The standards are, therefore, grouped in three levels: Essential, Very Desirable, and Desirable. Each proposed requirement is judged based on its importance and the feasibility of attaining it.

The statements listed as Essential are intended to represent the consensus of present-day thinking concerning what is normally required for competent use of a test. Any test or testing situation may present some unique problems; it is undesirable for the standards to be treated as unduly rigid; for example, they should not bind the producer of a novel test to an inappropriate procedure or form of reporting. The Essential standards indicate what information or practices will be needed for most tests in most applications. When a test developer or test user fails to satisfy these requirements, he should do so only as a considered judgment. In any single test or testing situation, there may be some Essential standards that do not apply. It should be noted that many of these standards require thought rather than specific action as an outcome of thought; for example, "A test user should consider...." In most cases, such statements are listed as Essential.

If some type of Essential information is not available on a given test, it is important to help the reader recognize that the research on the test is incomplete in this respect. A test manual should include clear statements of what research has been done and avoid misleading statements.

The category Very Desirable is used to draw attention to types of information or practices that contribute greatly to the user's understanding of the test and to competence in its use. Standards in this category have not been listed as Essential if their usefulness is debatable.

The category Desirable includes information and practices that are helpful but not Essential or Very Desirable.

When a test is widely used, the developer has a greater responsibility for investigating it thoroughly and providing more extensive reports about it than when the test is limited in use. Large sales make research financially possible. Therefore, the developer of a popular test can add information in subsequent editions of the manual. For tests having limited sales, it is unreasonable to expect that as much information will be furnished.

Cautions To Be Exercised in the Use of These Standards

Almost any test can be useful for some function and in some situations, but even the best test can have damaging consequences if used inappropriately. Therefore, the primary responsibility for the improvement of testing continues to rest on the shoulders of test users. It is hoped that these standards will be used to extend the professional training of many test users who are not now being trained appropriately. Professional training of personnel managers, school administrators, and classroom teachers should prepare them to better understand information about tests, test interpretations, and these standards. Such training will do much to improve the quality of test use and to minimize the extent of test misuse. The standards draw attention to recent developments in thinking about tests, test analysis, and test use. A comparison of these standards with those in earlier editions should remind test developers and test users that testing is a stable but not a static enterprise and that, in fact, there is room for improvement in the quality of assessments that are being made.

Tests are often developed and used in circumstances that lead to maintaining less than the highest standards of technical excellence. We do not intend to discourage those who must make assessments of people from doing the best they can with whatever training and collaborative resources are available to them. These standards, however, are written to promote excellence. They provide a kind of checklist of factors to be considered in designing, standardizing, validating, scoring, and interpreting tests. They may help test developers and test users decide what studies are needed and how those studies might best be recorded in manuals or in validation reports. Test users who are not going to do independent research on a test should refer to these standards for guidance in the choice, administration, scoring, and interpretation of tests.

It is conceivable that a test developer could fulfill most of the standards presented and still produce a test that would fall short of his intended or stated objectives. Care should be exercised to adhere, both in test development and test use, to the spirit as well as to the letter of these standards. Because of the possibility of misunderstanding or misinterpretation, it would not be appropriate for test developers or test users to state that a manual or procedure "satisfies" or "follows" these standards. There would be no objection to a statement that one has "taken into account or considered" these standards.

A final caveat is necessary in view of the prominence of testing issues in litigation. This document is prepared as a technical guide for those within the sponsoring professions; it is *not* written as law. What is intended is a set of standards to be used in part for self-evaluation by test developers and test users. An evaluation of their competence does not rest on the literal satisfaction of every relevant provision of this document. The individual standards are statements of ideals or goals, some having priority over others. Instead, an evaluation of competence depends on the degree to which the intent of this document has been satisfied by the test developer or user.

Tests vary in the amount of knowledge and research required to develop them. Much background work is needed for a test that is published or otherwise distributed for widespread use. Less work need be done for a test developed for local use. At any level, however, better tests and testing can be expected where test developers have been guided by fundamental considerations and have demonstrated this in writing.

A test user needs information describing a test's rationale, development, technical characteristics, administration, and interpretation. Such information is ordinarily expected in a test manual or in its supplements. This information is also needed by those using a test or test battery that has not been published but which is used within an organization to aid in making decisions. For these uses, a properly prepared manual reports to local users and to other interested persons (colleagues in other organizations, representatives of governmental agencies, representatives of citizen's groups, etc.) the procedures followed in construction of the test, in its use, and in the interpretation of scores derived from it. In certification or selection programs, a manual can present information about the program as a whole as well as about component tests. Data supporting claims for the program, procedures followed, kinds of tests used, and related information should be recorded not only to provide an adequate basis for the proper use of tests but also to make the information available for public scrutiny.

The development of a test or testing program is based on research; the report of that research is often contained in a manual. These standards, therefore, concentrate on the manual (and any supplementary publication) as the full and proper report of what was done in test development; they specify standards of reporting from which one may infer standards for research.

A. Dissemination of Information

A test user needs information to help him use the test in standard ways and to evaluate a test relative to others he might select for a given purpose. The information that he needs to select a test or to use it must come, at least in part, from the test developer. Practices of authors and publishers in furnishing information have varied. Sometimes the test manual offers only vague directions for administering and scoring, norms of uncertain origin, and perhaps nothing more. In contrast, some manuals furnish extensive information on test development, validity, reliability, bases for normative information, appropriate kinds of interpretations and uses, and they present all such information in detail.

A1.   When a test is published or otherwise made available for operational use, it should be accompanied by a manual (or other published or readily available

information) that makes every reasonable effort to follow the recommendations of these standards and, in
particular, to provide the information
required to substantiate any claims that
have been made for its use. Essential

[Comment: The term "operational
use" refers to making practical
decisions about the evaluation or
handling of individuals, groups,
curricula, therapeutic treatments, and
so on.

The term "manual" refers to
documents describing procedures of
test development, use, interpretation,
relevant research, normative data, and
related information. Depending on
such things as the amount of
information to report and the diversity
of uses and users, the term may
designate a document entirely within
one cover or a series of separately
bound pamphlets. This term might also
be extended to include procedural
manuals governing the use of tests or of
test batteries in, for example, selection
situations; the wording and importance
of many of these standards would be
different for a procedural manual, but
the principles applicable to test
manuals would at least, therefore, be
analogous.

Not all of the standards in this report
will apply to any one particular test. A
standard may be ignored if it is
irrelevant in light of the purpose of the
test and the claims made for it, but it
may not be ignored merely because it is
difficult to meet or has not usually been
met by a similar test.]

A1.1. If information needed to
support interpretations suggested in the
manual cannot be presented at the time
the manual is published, the manual
should satisfy the intent of standard A1
by pointing out the absence and
importance of this information.
Essential

A1.2. Where the information is too
extensive to be fully reported in the
manual, the essential information
should be summarized and
accompanied by references to other
sources of information, such as
technical supplements, articles, or
books. Very Desirable

[Comment: Developers of some well-
known tests provide extensive technical
manuals, make further research data
available through other sources (such as
the Education Resources Information
Center), prepare annotated bibliog-
raphies, or include relevant information
in technical books which users are
encouraged to consult. In other instances, the essential information is
given in the manual sold with the
instrument, along with references to
other useful sources.

Publications by persons other than
the author of the test frequently fulfill
many functions of a manual. If a book
about a test is designed to serve as a
manual, its author and publisher have
the same responsibility in preparing it
as do the author and publisher of a
test.]

A1.2.1. When information about a
test is provided in a separate
publication, that publication should
meet the same standards of accuracy
and freedom from misleading impressions that apply to the manual.
Essential

A1.2.2. Promotional material for a

test should be accurate and should not give the reader false impressions. Essential

[Comment: One publisher presents an extensive and complete bibliography, without comment or annotation, of research involving a test; he does *not* mention that many of the entries are studies with negative findings. The impression is one of extensive use, not of limitations to the usefulness of the test.]

A1.2.3. Informational material distributed within a using organization should be accurate, complete for the purposes of the reader's need, and written in language that will not give the reader a false impression. Essential

[Comment: Such information is often given in brief memoranda. In preparing these brief reports, the technical capability of the readers may be kept in mind, but this does not suggest that essential information be either omitted or distorted in the interest of simplicity. Where a reader may be expected to receive such reports regularly, efforts can be made to increase his ability to understand technical detail.]

A2. **A test manual should describe fully the development of the test: the rationale, specifications followed in writing items or selecting observations, and procedures and results of item analysis or other research. Essential**

A2.1. Data gathered during the process of developing a test before it is in final form should be clearly distinguished from data pertaining to the test in final form. Essential

A2.2. A test manual should specify the need for maintaining necessary test security. Very Desirable

[Comment: For example, a manual might describe some acceptable coaching practices. If so, it would be appropriate to add warnings against unacceptable practices that might jeopardize test security.]

A2.3. A test manual or supplementary document should provide representative sample items and a statement of the intended purpose of the test in a form that can be made available to those concerned about the nature and quality of a testing program. Very Desirable

[Comment: The evaluation of a test may not fall exclusively to those who are technically trained. Examinees, members of citizen panels, civil rights advocates, and parents are among those who may have reason to make judgments about the appropriateness of a test. Their right to do so need not conflict with the necessity to maintain test security if descriptive and explanatory materials are made available.

One publisher of educational tests has published descriptive material in nontechnical language for a wide variety of tests; pamphlets include information on test development and rationale as well as examples of items and suggestions on test-taking strategies.]

A2.4. The identity and professional qualifications of item writers and editors should be described in instances where they are relevant; for example, when adequacy of coverage of a subject-matter achievement test cannot appropriately or practically be measured against any external criterion. Desirable

A3. The test and its manual should be revised at appropriate intervals. The time for revision has arrived whenever changing conditions of use or new research data make any statements in the manual incorrect or misleading. Very Desirable

[Comment: The technical characteristics and the appropriateness of a test may change as social conditions and attitudes, job definitions, educational pressures, or the composition of relevant school populations change.]

A3.1. Competent studies of the test following its publication, whether the results are favorable or unfavorable to the test, should be taken into account in revised editions of the manual or its supplementary reports. Pertinent studies by investigators other than the test authors and publishers should be included. Very Desirable

[Comment: The developer of one test has published a comprehensive review of validity studies of the test covering a 15-year period.]

A3.2. When the test is revised or a new form is issued, the manual should be suitably revised to take those changes into account. In addition, the nature and extent of the revision and the comparability of data from the old test and the revised test should be explicitly stated. Essential

[Comment: It is useful for publishers to identify revisions of test manuals in their catalogs and to take other steps to increase the probability that test users have current information.]

A3.2.1. If a short form of a test is prepared by reducing the number of items or organizing a portion of the test into a separate form, new evidence should be obtained and reported for that shorter test. Essential

[Comment: It is especially important to report the reliability and other technical data for the test in its shorter form, since placing items in a new context may alter responses to them.

In the manual for one test that has two alternate forms, the validity data presented were obtained using the sum of the scores of the two forms. It would have been more appropriate to have presented the data for each form independently.]

A3.2.2. When a short form is prepared from an established test, the manual should present evidence that the items in the short form represent the items in the long form or measure the same characteristics as the long form. Very Desirable

[Comment: When no short form of a test has been prepared but there is reason to believe that it is commonly used in a shortened form, the manual should remind the reader that data in the manual may not be applicable to results of administration of a shortened form.

One revision of a long-established achievement test battery illustrates a desirable practice by listing all previous editions and then describing in detail the relation of the new revision to the previous editions.]

B. Aids to Interpretation

The responsibility for making inferences about the meaning and legitimate uses of test results rests primarily with the user. In making such judgments, however, he must depend in part on information about the test made available by its developer.

The manual or report form from a scoring service cannot fully prepare the user for interpreting the test. He will sometimes have to make judgments that have not been substantiated by published evidence. Thus, the vocational counselor cannot expect to have validity data available for each job about which he makes tentative predictions from test scores. The counselor or employment interviewer will have examinees who do not fit into any group for which normative or validity data are available. The teacher will have to evaluate the content of an achievement test in terms of his instructional goals and emphasis. The clinician must bring general data and theory into his interpretation of data from a personality inventory. The degree to which the manual can be expected to prepare the user for accurate interpretation and effective use of the test varies with the type of test and the purpose for which it is used. It is the test developer's responsibility to provide the information necessary for good judgment; in fact, developers should make tests as difficult to misuse and to misinterpret as they can.

B1. **The test, the manual, the record forms, and other accompanying material should help users make correct interpretations of the test results and should warn against common misuses.** Essential

B1.1. Names given to published tests, and to parts within tests, should be chosen to minimize the risk of misinterpretation by test purchasers and subjects. Essential

[Comment: It is desirable that names carry no unwarranted suggestion as to the characteristics measured. Such descriptions as "culture-free," "intelligence," "introversion," "creativity," "primary mental abilities," or "productivity quotients" are questionable for published tests, unless there is appropriate evidence of construct validity, since they may suggest interpretations going beyond the demonstrable meaning of the scores.]

B1.1.1. Devices for identifying interests and personality traits through self-report should be entitled "inventories," "questionnaires," or "checklists" rather than "tests." Very Desirable

[Comment: In referring to such instruments in textual material, however, as in these standards, the word "test" may be used to simplify the language even where it is properly avoided in the title.]

B1.2. The manual should draw the user's attention to data that especially need to be taken into account in the interpretation of test scores. Very Desirable

[Comment: Many test manuals point out variables that should be considered in the interpretation of a test score, such as information about school record, recommendations, or clinically relevant history.

A personality assessment manual may provide data to show that the psychologist should consider such facts as the sex and age of the subject, whether his parents are dead or separated, the ages and sexes of his siblings, or his vocational or marital status.]

B1.3. The manual should call attention to marked influences on test scores known to be associated with region, socioeconomic status, race, creed, color, national origin, or sex. Essential

[Comment: Social or cultural factors known to affect performance on the test differentially, administrator errors that are frequently repeated, examiner-examinee differences, and other factors that may result in spurious or unfair test scores should, for example, be clearly and prominently identified in the manual.]

B1.4. The manual should draw attention to, and warn against, any serious error of interpretation that is known to be frequent. Essential

[Comment: Some users of general intelligence tests think of the score as a direct measure of inherent native ability, given and unchanging; manuals of such tests may be expected to caution against this interpretation and to do so with reference to appropriate data. They should clearly warn users against unwarranted assumptions about the generality of normative data, particularly avoiding the impression that national norms are genuinely representative when in fact they are not. Manuals for interest inventories can apply this standard by stressing the fact

that interest does not necessarily imply ability and is only one of many factors to be considered in choosing among occupations.]

B2. **The test manual should state explicitly the purposes and applications for which the test is recommended.** Essential

[Comment: A clear statement of a test's purposes will help prevent the misapplication of test scores. It will alert the user to the kind and extent of evidence he should expect to find in the manual in support of the claims made for the test by the author and publisher. For example, if an achievement test is recommended as a survey test of what students know, an accurate description of its content is important. If, on the other hand, it is recommended as a diagnostic test or one that predicts performance, data on its relationship with one or more criteria are required. See Section E on validity.]

B2.1. If a test is intended for research use only and is not distributed for operational use, that fact should be prominently stated in the accompanying materials. Essential

[Comment: If the developer of a new device (e.g., for studying personality) releases his instrument for studies by other investigators before he considers it ready for operational use, it is appropriate to print "distributed for research use only" on the test package, on the cover of the booklet of directions, and in any catalog where it is listed. This cautions against premature use of the instrument in guidance or selection.]

B3. The test manual should describe clearly the psychological, educational, or other reasoning underlying the test and nature of the characteristic it is intended to measure. Essential

[Comment: There ordinarily are explicit reasons for setting up the test as it has been done; it may be assumed that certain psychological processes are required in taking the test and that certain traits are being measured as a result. The identification of these processes may be based on a theory, empirical research, or empirical processes internal to the test itself. In any case, a clear description of the construct or content and of the manner of measurement enables a user to judge the test by its conformity to his own psychological or educational insight as well as by statistical evidence of its efficacy.]

B3.1. In the case of tests developed for content-referenced interpretation, special attention should be given to defining the content domain in operational terms. In the case of a mastery test, the test developer's rationale for any cutting score that he suggests should be specified, or the procedures that the user might employ to establish mastery levels should be described. Essential

[Comment: The test user needs such information so that he can compare his concept of mastery or competence with that of the test author.]

B4. The test manual should identify any special qualifications required to administer the test and to interpret it properly. Essential

[Comment: One manual differentiates psychologists who work with children from those who work only with adults in identifying qualifications needed to use an individually administered test for children. Another offers specifications for administering the test to non-English-speaking students.

User qualifications might be described in terms of special training generally thought necessary to achieve competence. It may be possible for some test manuals to identify the most frequent sources of error in test use and to specify the kind of user training necessary to eliminate these common errors.

B4.1. The test manual should not imply that a test is "self-interpreting." It should specify information to be given about test results to persons who lack the training usually required to interpret them. Essential

[Comment: It is not ordinarily desirable to entrust interpretation of scores to an untrained person. There are, of course, tests that can be scored by the examinee, and it is often useful to give scores to students or parents. Where these practices are followed, the sense of this standard is that interpretative aids should also be given.

The manual should indicate what may be done by untrained persons and what should not be done. The manual for one well-known interests test, for example, indicates that examinees may perform the mechanics of scoring their own tests but properly stresses that they need the help of a trained teacher or counselor in making interpretations and future plans.]

B4.2. Where a test is recommended for a variety of purposes or types of inference, the manual should indicate the amount of training required for each use. Essential

B4.3. The manual should draw the user's attention to references with which he should become familiar before attempting to interpret the test results. Very Desirable

[Comment: The references might be to books or articles dealing with related psychological theory or with the particular test in question.]

B5. Evidence of validity and reliability, along with other relevant research data, should be presented in support of any claims being made. Essential

[Comment: Standards for validity and reliability are extensive. Moreover, they are as applicable to research reports prepared by test users as to test manuals. For these reasons, and because of their overreaching importance, a major section of this document presents standards for reports of research on validity and reliability. Adherence to the intent of this standard requires adherence to the appropriate standards in that section.]

B5.1. Statements in the manual reporting relationships are by implication quantitative and should be stated as precisely as the data permit. If data to support such statements have not been collected, that fact should be made clear. Essential

[Comment: Writers sometimes say, for example, "Spatial ability is required for architectural engineering," or,

"Bizarre responses may indicate schizophrenic tendencies." Such statements by themselves are quantitatively inadequate. In what proportion of cases giving bizarre responses has schizophrenia been shown to develop? How much has architectural success been found to depend upon spatial ability? Numerical data relating the test scores to definite criteria would help to provide the answers.]

B5.2. Statistical procedures that are well known and readily interpreted should be preferred for reporting any quantitative information. Any uncommon statistical techniques should be explained, and references to descriptions of them should be given. Essential

[Comment: Publishers need not uniformly adhere to the procedures commonly used for reporting data, but terminology and procedures should be sufficiently common in practice to permit adequate judgment by reasonably competent users.

This standard is an elaboration of the principle that data presented in a manual should not be misleading. For example, it is misleading to show the value of combining tests in a battery in a regression equation by using data where intercorrelations are lower than those reported elsewhere in the manual.]

B5.3. When the statistical significance of a relationship is reported, the statistical report should be in a form that makes clear the sensitivity or power of the significance test. Essential

[Comment: Statistical significance

that has no practical usefulness can often be obtained by using a very large number of cases. For example, a well-known inventory yields statistically significant differences between large samples of males and of females, but the differences are too small to be of practical importance. Conversely, one who uses an insensitive statistical test can falsely conclude that there is no difference of practical importance. In general, it is more appropriate in reporting test data to state a confidence interval or the likelihood function for the parameter of interest than to report only that the null hypothesis can or cannot be rejected.]

B5.4. The manual should differentiate between an interpretation that is applicable only to average tendencies of a group and one that is applicable to an individual within the group. Very Desirable

B5.5. The manual should state clearly what interpretations are intended for each subscore as well as for the total test. Essential

[Comment: Where subscores are obtained only for convenience in scoring the test, and no interpretation is intended, this should be made clear. For some tests, keys are provided for subscores that have possible research use but are not intended to be interpreted; this should be made clear.]

B6. Test developers or others offering computer services for test interpretation should provide a manual reporting the rationale and evidence in support of computer-based interpretations of scores. Essential

[Comment: A computer makes possible the storage and recall of large amounts of data; test interpretation can be greatly assisted by the use of computer data banks. Computer scoring services may provide lengthy printouts of descriptive and prognostic information from individual profiles on a test battery or personality inventory. The user of such printouts needs to know the reasoning and the evidence supporting the suggested interpretations because they are as fallible as other subjective interpretations.]

C. Directions for Administration and Scoring

Interpretations of test and measurement techniques, like those of experimental results, are most reliable when the measurements are obtained under standardized or controlled conditions. To be sure, there are circumstances in testing where it may be important to change conditions systematically for maximum understanding of the performance of an individual. For example, an examiner may systematically modify procedures in successive readministrations of a test to explore the limits of a child's mastery of a specific content area such as a set of concepts. Nevertheless, the test developer should provide a standard procedure from which modifications can be made. Without standardization, the quality of interpretations will be reduced to whatever extent differences in procedure influence performance.

For most purposes, great emphasis is properly placed on strict standardization of procedures for administering a test and reciting its instructions. If a test is to be used for a wide range of subpopulations, these procedures should be wholly comprehensible to all examinees in each subpopulation.

C1. The directions for administration should be presented in the test manual with sufficient clarity and emphasis so that the test user can duplicate, and will be encouraged to duplicate, the administrative conditions under which the norms and the data on reliability and validity were obtained. Essential

[Comment: Because persons administering tests in schools and industry sometimes may not follow instructions rigidly and may not understand the need for doing so, it is necessary that the manual be insistent and persuasive on this point. Some tests are fully administered by tape recordings to insure standardization of procedure.]

C1.1. The directions published in the test manual should be complete enough that persons tested will understand the task as the author intended. Essential

[Comment: For example, in a personality inventory, it may be intended that the subject give the first response that occurs to him. If so, this expectation should be made clear in the directions read by or to the subject. Directions for interest inventories should specify whether the person is to mark what things he would ideally like to do or whether he is also to consider the possibility that he would have the opportunity and ability to do them. Likewise, the directions should specify whether the person is to mark those things he would like to do and does oc-

casionally, or only those things he would like to do and does regularly.]

C1.1.1. The directions should clearly point out such critical matters as instructions on guessing, time limits, and procedures for marking answer sheets. Essential

C1.1.2. The directions to the test administrator should include guidance for dealing with questions from examinees. Very Desirable

C1.2. If expansion or elaboration of instructions described in the test manual is permitted, the conditions under which this may be done should be clearly stated either in the form of general rules or in terms of giving numerous examples, or both. Essential

C2. Instructions should prepare the examinee for the examination: Sample material, practice use of answer sheets or punch cards, sample questions, etc., should be provided. Desirable

[Comment: The extent and nature of such material depends on expected levels of knowledge among examinees. For example, extensive practice material might be wasteful if developed for frequently tested school children and for a commonly encountered type of test; it may be very important for a novel test format to be administered to older job applicants.]

C3. The procedures for scoring the test should be presented in the test manual with a maximum of detail and clarity to reduce the likelihood of scoring error. Essential

C3.1. The test manual should furnish scoring instructions that maximize the accuracy of scoring an objective test by outlining a procedure for checking the obtained scores for computational or clerical errors. Very Desirable

C3.2. Where subjective processes enter into the scoring of a test, evidence on the degree of agreement between independent scorings under operational conditions should be presented in the test manual. If such evidence is not provided, the manual should draw attention to scoring variations as a possible significant source of errors of measurement. Very Desirable

C3.2.1. The bases for scoring and the procedures for training scorers should be presented in the test manual in sufficient detail to permit other scorers to reach the level of agreement reported in studies of scorer agreement given in the manual. Very Desirable

C3.2.2. If persons having various degrees of supervised training are expected to score the test, studies of the interscorer agreement at each skill level should be presented in the test manual. Desirable

C3.3. If the test is designed to use more than one method for the examinee's recording of his reponses, such as hand-scored answer sheets, or entering of responses in the test booklet, the test manual should report data on the degree to which results from these methods are interchangeable. Essential

[Comment: The different amounts of time required for responding to items in forms adapted to different scoring methods may affect the reliability or validity of the test or the applicability of the test norms.]

C3.4. If an unusual or complicated scoring system is used, the test manual should indicate the approximate amount of time required to score the test. Desirable

C3.5. "Correction-for-guessing" formulas should be used with multiple-choice and true-false items when the test is speeded. Desirable

D. Norms and Scales

Interpretations of test scores traditionally have been *norm referenced*; that is, an individuals score is interpreted in terms of comparisons with scores made by other individuals. Alternative interpretations are possible.- *Content-referenced* interpretations are those where the score is directly interpreted in terms of performance at each point on the achievement continuum being measured. *Criterion-referenced* interpretations are those where the score is directly interpreted in terms of performance at any given point on the continuum of an *external* variable. An external criterion variable might be grade averages or levels of job performance.[2]

[2]Current usage in educational measurement commonly refers to "criterion-referenced" interpretations for *both* alternatives to interpretations requiring norms. The different meanings of the word "criterion," however, produce some confusion; some measurement specialists have therefore turned to the term "content referenced" and this usage is adopted here. The word "criterion," as it is used in the phrase "criterion-related" validity (that is, an external variable) has suggested a similar but distinguishable alternative to normative interpretation; therefore, "content-referenced and criterion-referenced" are not interchangeable terms as used in this document.)

The standards in this section refer principally to tests intended for norm-referenced test interpretations rather than for content-referenced interpretations.

D1. Norms should be published in the test manual at the time of release of the test for operational use. Essential

D1.1. Norms should be established even for a test developed only for local use or only for predictive purposes. Desirable

[Comment: It is sometimes forgotten that norms tables provide information useful for purposes other than comparing one individual with group data. For example, a test user can derive information from a normative table about the score levels at which the discrimination power of the measurement is good or poor.]

D1.2. Even though a test is expected to be used primarily with local norms, the test manual should nevertheless provide normative data to aid the interpreter who lacks local norms. Very Desirable

[Comment: The manual for one instrument designed to measure employee aptitude stresses the value of local norms but also includes norms based on a wide variety of occupational and educational classifications.]

D2. Norms presented in the test manual should refer to defined and clearly described populations. These populations should be the groups with whom users of the test will ordinarily wish to compare the persons tested. Essential

[Comment: It should be noted that "populations" are plural; in nearly all instances of tests developed for other than purely local use, the user needs to know the applicability of the test to different groups. For tests developed with a view to widespread use in schools or industry, information is needed about differences or similarities of normative data for appropriate subgroups such as sex, ethnic, grade, or age groups. Users need to be alert to situations when norms are less extensive for one group than another.

For example, the manual for an occupational interest inventory, or for an aptitude test particularly useful in certain occupations, should point out that a person who has a high degree of interest or aptitude in a curriculum or occupation when compared to people in general will usually have a lower degree of interest or aptitude compared to persons actually engaged in that field. Thus, a high percentile score on a scale reflecting musical interest, in which the examinee is compared with people in general, may be equivalent to a low percentile where the examinee is compared with professional musicians.]

D2.1. Care should be taken to avoid misleading impressions about the generality of normative data. Essential

[Comment: Truly representative national norms, for example, are rarely if ever obtained; normative data collected from people or schools with specific characteristics, however, are frequently used as if they were taken from a representative national group. Thus, we have test users who may say that an examinee's performance is at a "tenth-grade reading level," without qualification when the norms are in fact obtained only from superior schools voluntarily participating in the test research. It is an error of interpretation to assume that the norms of the volunteer group of schools apply to schools in general; the incidence of such erros may be reduced by manuals that clearly define the characteristics of the normative populations.]

D2.1.1. The test manual should report the method of sampling from the population of examinees and should discuss any probable bias in this sampling procedure. Essential

D2.1.2. Norms reported in any test manual should be based on well-planned samplings rather than on data collected primarily because it is readily available. Any deviations from the plan should be reported along with descriptions of actions taken or not taken with respect to them. Essential

[Comment: Occupational and educational test norms have often been based on scattered groups of test papers, for authors sometimes have requested that all users mail in results for use in subsequent reports of norms. Distributions so obtained are subject to unknown degrees and types of biases. Hence, the methods of obtaining such samples should be clearly described.]

D2.1.3. In addition to reporting the number of individuals in a set of normative data, the manual should also report the number of sampling units from which those individuals were drawn along with the numbers of individuals in each unit. Essential

D2.2. The description of the norms group in the test manual should be complete enough so that the user can judge its appropriateness for his use. The description should include number of cases, classified by one or more of such relevant variables as ethnic mix, socioeconomic level, age, sex, locale, and educational status. If cluster sampling is employed, the description of the norms group should state the number of separate groups tested. Essential

[Comment: Manuals often use too gross a classification system in describing their normative data. For example, the manual for one employee aptitude test provides a variety of normative data for many occupational and educational groupings. However, the lack of information as to sex, ethnic origins, age, education, and experience levels within these groupings considerably reduces the usefulness of the norms.]

D2.2.1. The populations upon which the psychometric properties of a test were determined and for which normative data are available should be *clearly and prominently described* in the manual. Any accompanying report forms should provide space for identifying the normative groups used in interpreting the scores. Essential

[Comment: The intent of this standard is to provide a warning to consumers (users and examinees) against unwarranted interpretations. If a standard report form results in percentile-rank or standard-score interpretations by consistently using the same normative population, the definition of that population, with an indication of the time period of data collection, would be sufficient.]

D2.3. If the sample on which norms are based is small or otherwise undependable, the user should be cautioned explicitly in the test manual regarding the possible magnitude of errors arising in the interpretation of scores. Very Desirable

D2.4. Norms on subtests or groups of test items should be reported in the test manual only if the validity and reliability of such subtests or groups of items are also indicated. Essential

[Comment: The test user is justified in assuming that, when norms are given for part of a test, the author implies their usefulness for interpreting performance. The reliability and validities of such scores should be reported.]

D2.5. The significant aspects of conditions under which normative data were obtained should be reported in the test manual. Essential

[Comment: Some tests are standardized on job-applicant groups, others on groups that have requested vocational guidance, and, still others, on groups that realized that they were experimental subjects. While precise description of levels is probably not always possible, motivation for taking tests, test-taking attitudes, abilities, and personality characteristics often differ within these groups and from group to group.]

D3. In reporting norms, test manuals should use percentiles for one or more appropriate reference groups or standard scores for which the basis is clearly set forth; any exceptional type of score or unit should be explained and justified. Measures of central tendency and variability always should be reported. Essential

D3.1. In the case of tests used for prediction, expectancy tables or experience tables translating obtained scores into probabilities of success or into proficiency levels should be included whenever possible. Desirable

D4. Local norms are more important for many uses of tests than are published norms. A test manual should suggest using local norms in such situations. Very Desirable

D5. Derived scales used for reporting scores should be carefully described in the test manual to increase the likelihood of accurate interpretation of scores by both the test interpreter and the examinee. Essential

[Comment: It would be helpful if the number of kinds of derived scales could be reduced to a few with which testers can become familiar. The present variety makes description necessary in each manual. In part the problem is that many different systems are now used that have no logical advantage over others; some may have outlived their usefulness. New scaling methods may be used in attempts to overcome presumed difficulties with older ones. The variety of scales for reporting test scores can create confusion and misinterpretation unless the scales recommended for a given test are clearly and fully explained.]

D5.1. Derivation of any scale from normative data should be clearly and unambiguously described in terms likely to prevent user misinterpretations or overgeneralization. Essential

[Comment: Derived scores can be very useful for drawing inferences. Too often, however, they are treated as if they had absolute meaning independent of a particular test or normative population. An example is the IQ; it is often simply a standard score, but it is frequently reified and interpreted as representing an unchanging and unchangeable characteristic of the person tested. Grade-equivalent scores or even percentile ranks may also be misinterpreted as absolute entities unless the manual makes clear the reference group on which they were based.]

D5.2. When standard scores are used, the system should be consistent with the purposes for which the test is intended and should be described in detail in the test manual. The reasons for choosing one scale in preference to another should also be made clear in the manual. Very Desirable

D5.2.1. The manual should specify whether standard scores are linear transformations of raw scores or are normalized. Essential

D5.2.2. The choice of a standard scale should be based upon either the standard error of measurement of raw scores or on some other basis that is clearly defined. Desirable

[Comment: There are many standard-score scales in use. The scale for reporting scores on one widely used test is so designed that each unit of the scale is equal to about one thirtieth of the overall standard error of measurement; a different test used for similar purposes is scaled so that one unit is equal to about one third the overall standard error of measurement. The former scale suggests a greater degree of precision than the latter, but this implication is unwarranted.]

D5.2.3. Interpretive scores that lend themselves to gross misinterpretations, such as mental-age or grade-equivalent scores, should be abandoned or their use discouraged. Very Desirable

[Comment: When, despite this recommendation, such scores are included in a manual, their relationship to standard scores or percentile ranks, within each category and within an appropriate norm group, should also be provided in tabular form. For example, the table might show, in addition to a grade-equivalent score, the corresponding percentile rank within the examinee's own age or grade level for each raw score. At the high school level, norms within courses (for example, second-year Spanish) may be more appropriate than norms within grades.]

D5.3. When it is suggested in the test manual that percentile ranks are to be plotted on a profile sheet, the profile sheet should be based on the normal probability scale or some other appropriate nonlinear transformation. Very Desirable

D5.4. Normative data should be provided in a form that emphasizes the fallibility of an obtained score. Very Desirable

[Comment: Some publishers provide norms showing ranges of standard scores or percentile ranks that have designated probability levels including the true score. A norms table might show for each raw score, not only the associated standard score or percentile rank but also the values for raw scores at plus and at minus one standard error of measurement for each raw score.

D6. If scales are revised, new forms added, or other changes made, the revised test manual should provide tables of equivalence between the new and the old forms. This provision is particularly important in cases where data are recorded on cumulative records. Desirable

[Comment: New forms of a test should be equated to *recently determined* standard-score scales of other forms, in order that the user may be confident that the scores furnished by the new forms are comparable with those of earlier forms.]

D6.1. When a new form is equated with an older form of a test, the revised manual should describe the content of both old and new forms and the nature of the norms group for each form. Essential

[Comment: Changes in knowledge, technology, or curricula may require that new editions of a test differ in

important respects from earlier editions, and the demand for continuity may require that the scales for reporting scores be equated. There is some doubt as to whether meaningful comparability of scores is possible with changed content, however, and a user should be able to evaluate claims of equivalency in terms of the kinds of content changes that have occurred.]

D6.2. The manual should describe the method used to establish equivalent or comparable scores and should include an assessment of the accuracy of the equating procedure. Very Desirable

D7. Where it is expected that a test will be used to assess groups rather than individuals (i.e., for schools or programs), normative data based on group summary statistics should be provided. Essential

[Comment: For example, it is inappropriate to evaluate schools by using norms developed for the evaluation of individuals. It is also inappropriate to compute group means for nonlinear scales such as percentile ranks derived for individual norms.

STANDARDS FOR REPORTS OF RESEARCH
ON RELIABILITY AND VALIDITY

A test developer must provide evidence of the reliability and validity of his test; it is usually reported in the test manual. Many test users should do similar research on their own application of the test. Their reports often differ from those in test manuals by being more detailed or more specific to a particular problem, or by validating test batteries rather than individual tests. Despite such differences, the standards of research, and of research reporting, should be generally similar in the two situations.

E. Validity

Questions of validity are questions of what may properly be inferred from a test score; validity refers to the appropriateness of inferences from test scores or other forms of assessment. The many types of validity questions can, for convenience, be reduced to two: (*a*) What can be inferred about what is being measured by the test? (*b*) What can be inferred about other behavior?

The first question inquires into the intrinsic nature of the measurement itself. The measuring instrument is an operational definition of a specified domain of skill or knowledge, or of a trait, of interest to the test developer or user. The essential problem in this context is to reach some conclusion as to how faithfully the scores represent that domain, and it is appropriate to speak of the validity of the measurement.

The second question inquires into the usefulness of the measurement as an indicator of some other variable as a predictor of behavior. In this context, the essential problem is to reach some conclusion about how well scores on the test are related to some other performance, and it is appropriate to speak of the closeness of the relationship.

The two questions are not necessarily independent. For example, where the test is a sample of the "other behavior," the answer is the same for either question. Moreover, answers to both questions may require a knowledge of the interrelationships between the test scores and other variables. A thorough understanding of validity may require many investigations. The investigative processes of gathering or evaluating the necessary data are called validation. There are various methods of validation, and all, in a fundamental sense, require a definition of what is to be inferred from the scores and data to show that there is an acceptable basis for such inferences.

It is important to note that validity is itself inferred, not measured. Validity coefficients may be presented in a manual, but validity for a particular aspect of test use is inferred from this collection of coefficients. It is, therefore, something that is *judged* as adequate, or marginal, or unsatisfactory.

The kinds of validity depend upon the kinds of inferences one might wish to draw from test scores. Four interdependent kinds of inferential interpretation are traditionally described to summarize most test use: the *criterion-related* validities (*predictive* and *concurrent*); *content* validity; and *construct* validity.[3] (So-called "face" validity, the mere appearance of validity, is not an acceptable basis for interpretive interferences from test scores.)

These aspects of validity can be discussed independently, but only for convenience. They are interrelated operationally and logically; only rarely is one of them alone important in a particular situation. A thorough study of a test may often involve information about all types of validity. In developing or choosing a test for prediction, one should first postulate the constructs likely to provide a basis for useful prediction of the variable of interest; the measures chosen should have adequate construct validity. The content universe from which items are sampled may also be an important early step in producing a predictive test, in evaluating a test considered for use as a predictor, or in developing the criterion measure to be predicted. Even if the accuracy of prediction is good, information about construct validity may make a test more useful. To

evaluate construct validity, all knowledge regarding validity is relevant. A reading comprehension test, for example, may be used and validated for all three types of inference: how well it predicts future academic performance, how well it samples a defined content area of material to read, and how well it measures the construct of comprehension.

Criterion-Related Validities

Criterion-related validities apply when one wishes to infer from a test score an individual's most probable standing on some other variable called a criterion. Statements of predictive validity indicate the extent to which an individual's future level on the criterion can be predicted from a knowledge of prior test performance; statements of concurrent validity indicate the extent to which the test may be used to estimate an individual's present standing on the criterion. The distinction is important. Predictive validity involves a time interval during which something may happen (e.g., people are trained, or gain experience, or are subjected to some treatment). Concurrent validity reflects only the status quo at a particular time. Under appropriate circumstances, data obtained in a concurrent study may be used to estimate the predictive validity of a test. However, concurrent validity should not be used as a substitute for predictive validity without an appropriate supporting rationale.

For many test uses, such as for selection decisions or assignment to treatment, predictive validity provides the appropriate model for evaluating the use of a test or test battery. In employment testing, for example, use of

---

[3]Many other terms have been used. Examples include synthetic validity, convergent validity, job-analytic validity, rational validity, and factorial validity. In general, such terms refer to specific procedures for evaluating validity rather than to new kinds of interpretive inferences. Any specially-named procedures, including these examples, should meet the standards of investigation contained in this section. These standards apply generally to the various statistics or procedures that might be used in support of one or more classes of inferences from test scores.

any procedure implies prediction to some degree. Whether one uses a carefully developed test or casual judgments of interviewers, their use for selection purposes assumes that applicants who obtain high scores will become better employees than applicants who obtain low scores.

Other forms of validity are not substitutes for criterion-related validity. In choosing a test to select people for a job, for example, an abundance of evidence of the construct validity of a test of flexibility in divergent thinking, or of the content validity of a test of elementary calculus, is of no predictive value without reason to believe that flexibility of thinking or knowledge of calculus aids performance on that job. The *model* of predictive validity should guide thinking about validity in such applications even where circumstances preclude an actual criterion-related validation study. Whatever other validity information a manual may include, one or more studies of criterion-related validity must be included for any test developed for prediction and for many tests intended for diagnosis; otherwise, such tests can only be regarded as experimental.

Many factors may make a single, obtained validity coefficient questionable. First, the conditions of a validation study are never exactly repeated. Rapidly changing conditions may limit the usefulness of a predictive study. The logic of predictive validation assumes that conditions existing at the start of the time sequence will exist again after the study is completed.

Second, the logic of criterion-related validity assumes that the criterion possesses validity. All too often, tests are validated against any available criterion with no corresponding investigation of the criterion itself. The merit of a criterion-related validity study depends on the appropriateness and quality of the criterion measure chosen. In applied research, the criterion should be chosen with reference to the problem at hand, and the test or other assessment technique should be chosen with reference to the criterion. If the study is done primarily to enhance understanding of what a test measures, criteria should be selected in terms of beliefs about the nature of the construct reflected by the test scores. In either case, the adequacy of the study depends on the adequacy of the criterion. Criterion-related validity studies based on the "criterion at hand," chosen more for availability than for a place in a carefully reasoned hypothesis, are to be deplored.

Third, the logic of criterion-related validity assumes that the sample is truly representative of the population for which the later inferences are to be drawn. In practice, samples are often nonrepresentative because of, for example, restricted range, preselection, or attrition before a predictive study can be completed.

Fourth, in many practical situations validity studies cannot be done with adequate numbers of cases, and the investigators must do the best they can with the data at hand. It may be better to try to investigate criterion-related validity, even if imperfectly, than to accept totally untested hypotheses. However, "doing something" is not necessarily better than doing nothing; the results of an inadequate study may be quite misleading. Results of validation studies with severely restricted ranges or small Ns are especially open to question.

Content Validity

Evidence of content validity is required when the test user wishes to estimate how an individual performs in the universe of situations the test is intended to represent. Content validity is most commonly evaluated for tests of skill or knowledge; it may also be appropriate to inquire into the content validities of personality inventories, behavior checklists, or measures of various aptitudes. The present discussion will be directed toward the more typical case of achievement testing.

To demonstrate the content validity of a set of test scores, one must show that the behaviors demonstrated in testing constitute a representative sample of behaviors to be exhibited in a desired performance domain. Definitions of the performance domain, the users' objectives, and the method of sampling are critical to claims of content validity. An investigation of content validity requires that the test developer or test user specify his objectives and carefully define the performance domain in light of those objectives. The definition should ordinarily specify the results of learning rather than the processes by which learning is either sufficiently detailed and organized to show the degree to which component tasks make up the total domain.

Definition of the performance domain is relatively simple where it is finite and unambiguous, as in a simple test of addition for elementary-school use. Depending upon instructional objectives, the performance domain might be defined as *all* addition problems of three to five single-integer addends. The total number of problems and the relative frequency of occurrence of specific integers or pairs of integers within that total are known, and the representativeness of any sample of such problems can be easily judged.

If a test is used to estimate achievement in American history in Grade 12, the performance domain is less objectively defined. Given agreement on instructional objectives, it could be defined in terms of the types and quantities of the skills, facts, and concepts of American history, as determined by the pooled judgments of authorities, experienced teachers, and competent curriculum makers in that field. A definition of the total universe might well be tempered by the specific instructional objectives accepted by the panel. A definition appropriate for evaluation of performance at the end of the year of study would differ from the definition appropriate for developing an examination over knowledge of the colonial period. Within such limits, the performance domain requires definition so carefully detailed that rules for item writing will assure appropriate representation of all facets of the definition. It should be noted that an achievement test so constructed would not necessarily constitute a representative sample of the skills, facts, and concepts taught by any particular teacher during any particular year. Consequently, a definition of the performance domain of interest must always be provided by a test user so that the content of a test may be checked against an appropriate task universe.

It is appropriate to inquire into the content validity of many employment tests. Examples would include tests of typing skill, driving ability, or knowledge of certain regulatory laws. The performance domain for published tests might be defined by the pooled judgments of job designers, incumbents, and supervisors. Test users might define the performance domain of interest to them in terms of judgments of similar people in their own organizations or, preferably, in terms of appropriately detailed and comprehensive job analyses. The question of objectives would again enter into the definition; unless only fully trained and experienced people are to be hired, applicants cannot be expected to demonstrate proficiency in all facets of a job. The performance domain would need definition in terms of the objectives of measurement, restricted perhaps only to critical, most frequent, or prerequisite work behaviors.

It should be clear that content validity is quite different from face validity. Content validity is determined by a set of operations, and one evaluates content validity by the thoroughness and care with which these operations have been conducted. In contrast, face validity is a judgment that the requirements of a test merely *appear* to be relevant. The writing of items in terms used in a particular job or by a particular subgroup of the population may give an appearance of relevance while contributing nothing to content validity or indeed to any other useful validity information (although such items may serve a useful public-relations function).

In defining the content universe, a test developer or user is accountable for the adequacy of his definition. An employer cannot justify an employment test on grounds of content validity if he cannot demonstrate that the content universe includes all, or nearly all, important parts of the job.

Construct Validity

A psychological construct is an idea developed or "constructed" as a work of informed, scientific imagination; that is, it is a theoretical idea developed to explain and to organize some aspects of existing knowledge. Terms such as "anxiety," "clerical aptitude," or "reading readiness" refer to such constructs, but the construct is much more than the label; it is a dimension understood or inferred from its network of interrelationships.[4] It may be necessary to postulate several different constructs to account for the variance in any given set of test scores. Moreover, different constructs may be required to account for the variance in different tests of the same general type, or a given test may provide evidence relating to several constructs. For example, given proper evidence, scores on vocabulary tests might be used to infer (a) the level of present vocabulary; (b) the existence of pathology, interests, or values; or (c) intellectual capacity.

Construct validity is implied when one evaluates a test or other set of operations in light of the specified construct. Judgments of construct

---

[4]This is an admittedly restricted statement of the nature of scientific constructs, which may include entities as well as dimensions. Constructs of interest in the present context are, however, primarily quantitative.

validity are useful in efforts to improve measures for the scientific study of a construct. They are also useful when a test developer or test user wishes to learn more about the psychological qualities being measured by a test than can be learned from a single criterion-related validity coeffficient.

Evidence of construct validity is not found in a single study; rather, judgments of construct validity are based upon an accumulation of research results. In obtaining the information needed to establish construct validity, the investigator begins by formulating hypotheses about the characteristics of those who have high scores on the test in contrast to those who have low scores. Taken together, such hypotheses form at least a tentative theory about the nature of the construct the test is believed to be measuring. In a full investigation, the test may be the dependent variable in some studies and the independent variable in others. Some hypotheses may be "counterhypotheses" suggested by competing interpretations or theories.

Such hypotheses or theoretical formulations lead to certain predictions about how people at different score levels on the test will behave on certain other tests or in certain defined situations. If the investigator's theory about what the test measures is essentially correct, most of his predictions should be confirmed. If they are not, he may revise his definition of the construct, or he may revise the test to make it a better measure of the construct he had in mind. Through the process of successive verification, modification, or elimination of hypo-

theses, the investigator increases his understanding of the qualities measured by the test. Through the process of confirmation or disconfirmation, test revision, and new research on the revised instrument, he improves the usefulness of the test as a measure of a construct.

It is important to note in this that the investigation of construct validity refers to a specific test and not necessarily to any other test given the same label.

Evidence of construct validity may also be inferred from the procedures followed in developing a test. For example, in a measure of mechanical interest, a double item analysis may be used to reduce the effect of verbal ability. A preliminary item analysis might be done using a standard verbal-comprehension test as an external criterion. Those items with a very low discrimination index in this analysis could then be subjected to a second item analysis, a conventional internal-consistency analysis. Only those items with a low discrimination index in the first analysis and a high discrimination index in the second analysis would be included in the final item pool.

Although evidence of construct validity may be developed on the basis of a series of criterion-related studies, it is important to note that evidence of the construct validity of a test is *not* adequate evidence of the usefulness of the construct in specific further hypotheses. In the selection of salespersons, for example, it is often hypothesized that success is a function of sociability. If one has a measure of sociability with generally acceptable evidence of its validity as a measure of that construct, he may expect to find it useful as a predictor of sales success; perhaps some of the evidence of the construct validity of that measure came, in fact, from confirmation of such an expectation. However, the test may have no predictive validity against the criterion of success in an engineering sales job. In such a case it is not the construct validity of the sociability measure that is to be questioned.

General Principles

A test developer, or anyone who conducts validation research, should provide as much validity information as possible so the user can evaluate the test or the research for his own purposes. A test manual can provide evidence that will enable the user to evaluate the appropriateness of the item content, to determine whether the test is an acceptable measure of a specified construct, and to decide whether the test has provided useful predictive validities in situations similar to his own. An adequate research report can help the user decide whether to go ahead with the use of the test or to seek another predictor.

E1. A manual or research report should present the evidence of validity for each type of inference for which use of the test is recommended. If validity for some suggested interpretation has not been investigated, that fact should be made clear. Essential

[Comment: Validation studies are a part of the process of test development; test users expect them to be reported in detail by the developer, preferably in the manual itself. At the very least, the manual should summarize competent research reported elsewhere, either by the test developer or by others. Preferably, the manual will report on individual studies and provide summaries of validity data for various kinds of interpretations or inferences.]

E1.1. Statements about validity should refer to the validity of particular interpretations or of particular types of decisions. Essential

[Comment: It is incorrect to use the unqualified phrase "the validity of the test." *No test is valid for all purposes or in all situations or for all groups of individuals.* Any study of test validity is pertinent to only a few of the possible uses of or inferences from the test scores.

If the test is likely to be used incorrectly for certain areas of decision, the manual should include specific warnings. For example, the manual for a writing-skills test stated that the test apparently was not sufficiently difficult to discriminate among students "at colleges that have selective admissions."]

E1.2. Wherever interpretation of subscores, score differences, or profiles is suggested, the evidence justifying such interpretation should be made explicit. (See also B5.5.) Essential

E1.2.1. If the manual suggests that the user consider an individual's responses to specific items as a basis for assessment, it should either present evidence supporting this use or call attention to the absence of such data. The manual should warn the reader that inferences based on responses to single items are subject to extreme error. Hence, they should be used only to direct further inquiry, perhaps in a counseling interview. Essential

E1.3. To insure the continued correct interpretation of scores, the validity of suggested interpretations should be rechecked periodically; test developers should report results in subsequent editions of the manual. Very Desirable

[Comment: Job duties, conditions of work, and the types of individuals entering an occupation often change materially with the passage of time. Similarly, the meanings of clinical categories, the nature of therapeutic treatment, and the objectives of academic programs change. The difficulty and psychological meaning of test items will also change. Hence, the reader should be in a position to judge the extent to which tests are obsolete.]

E1.3.1. If factors that may affect test performance or the validity of a suggested test interpretation have changed, and validity studies have not been repeated for the changed conditions, the test should be withdrawn from general sale and distributed, if at all, only to persons who will conduct their own validity studies. Very Desirable

[Comment: It should be noted that no specific time interval is mentioned. Test developers and publishers should know the relevant conditions and should be able and willing to obtain new validity information when such conditions have changed. It is not necessary to repeat every part of the validation; what is needed is a repetition of those studies most likely to have been rendered obsolete. In the case of some inventories and biographical-data forms, scoring keys should be reevaluated after relatively brief periods of time.]

E1.4. Correlations of item scores with total scores on the test in which the item is included (or a parallel form of that test) may be presented as item-discrimination coefficients, but they should not be presented or used as item-validity coefficients. Essential

[Comment: Item-discrimination coeficients are useful in reasoning about construct validity, and such information is appropriately included in a manual. However, they are indicators of internal consistency, not of validity.]

E2. A test user is responsible for marshalling the evidence in support of his claims of validity and reliability. The use of test scores in decision rules should be supported by evidence. Essential

[Comment: It is a basic responsibility of a test user to read, understand, and evaluate the manual, the research, and the literature to show the appropriateness of the test for the intended use. A large-scale user may have the added responsibility for empirical research bearing on his claims of test validity. Evidence of validity is needed for *all* bases for decision, not merely those that are easy to study. It is a peculiar paradox that many employers and schools are abandoning the use of standardized tests and are turning instead to casual assessment techniques likely to be less valid. Many employers use procedures with no validity, or biased selection procedures of unknown validity rather than objective procedures for which evidence of validity could have been assembled.]

E2.1. Test users are responsible for gathering data on the validity and reliability of their assessment techniques. Very Desirable

[Comment: For many individual test users, this may be a nearly impossible requirement. It would seem, however, that a test user has an obligation to gather data, at least on an informal basis, in an effort to evaluate his work. In even the most difficult circumstances, a test user can be alert to data suggesting possible lack of validity.]

E2.2. If a user wants to use a test in a situation for which the use of the test has not been previously validated, or for which there is no supported claim for validity, he is responsible for validation. Very Desirable

[Comment: He who makes the claim for validity is responsible for providing the evidence. Evidence of validity sufficient for test use may often be obtained in a well-documented manual. If the test user wishes to claim that the validity generalizes beyond the evidence for the kinds of situations reported in the manual, it is his responsibility to demonstrate it.]

E2.3. When a test user plans to make a substantial change in test format, instructions, language, or content, he should revalidate the use of the tests for the changed conditions. Essential

Criterion-Related Validity

E3. All measures of criteria should be described completely and accurately. The manual or research report should comment on the adequacy of a criterion. Whenever feasible, it should draw attention to significant aspects of performance that the criterion measure does not reflect and to irrelevant factors likely to affect it. Essential

[Comment: Desirable practices are illustrated in a manual for a test designed to measure abstract intelligence. Several validity studies relating this instrument to criteria are reported, some involving concurrent measures and others involving predictions over periods of time. Limitations of the studies are recognized, and it is stated that "no one criterion is uniquely appropriate." The value of local norms is stressed, and an example of a local expectancy table is provided.

In the case of interest measures, it is sometimes not made clear whether the criterion indicates satisfaction, success, or merely continuance in the activity under examination. When criterion groups include people in a given occupation and when a comparison of such groups is made to people in general, the manual should point out the distinction between working in an occupation and success in it or satisfaction with it.]

E3.1. When the validity of a test for predicting occupational performance is reported, the manual should describe the duties of the workers as well as give their job titles. Very Desirable

[Comment: The principle is that information should be given from which the reader can make judgments of the relevance of the criterion. The description of a criterion is often incomplete without such information.]

E3.1.1. Where a wide range of duties is subsumed under a given occupational label, the test user should be warned against assuming that only one pattern of interests or abilities is compatible with the occupation. Essential

E4. A criterion measure should itself be studied for evidence of validity and that evidence should be presented in the manual or report. Very Desirable

[Comment: Criterion measures are forms of assessment and are subject to the same standards governing the development and use of any assessment technique. For many employment and educational purposes, the ideal criterion may be an achievement test or work sample judged acceptable in terms of content validity. Supervisory or instructor ratings are more common but may be questioned in terms of construct validity. For example, a rating of proficiency may be defined to include elements of both speed and accuracy, but to exclude elements of dependability. A judgment of acceptable construct validity might be based on evidence of high correlations of the ratings with production data or work samples and of independence from seniority or attendance data.]

E4.1. Particular attention should be given to potential sources of criterion contamination; results of investigations of contamination should be reported. Essential

[Comment: Results of such investigations are often ambiguous, and readers should be warned of this fact.

For example, an investigation of possible sex differences in criterion ratings might show significant differences between men and women. That fact in itself, however, is not sufficient evidence of criterion contamination; it might reflect actual sex differences in performance.]

E4.1.1. The criterion score should be determined independently of test scores. The manual should describe precautions taken to avoid contamination of the criterion or should warn the reader of possible contamination. Essential

[Comment: When the criterion is based on judgment, the manual should state whether the test data were available to the judge or were capable of influencing the judgments in any other way. If the test data could have influenced the criterion rating, the user should be warned that the reported validities are likely to be spuriously high.]

E4.2. The basis for judgments of criterion relevance should be clearly set forth. Essential

E.4.3. Criterion-related validation should ordinarily consider more than a single global criterion. Very Desirable

[Comment: In most situations where decision rules based on testing are worthwhile, performance falls along many dimensions that may be independent. Combining unrelated aspects of behavior into a single composite criterion may obscure important relationships and reduce a test user's opportunity to identify and understand valid test interpretations.

A problem exists in that single

instrument, and further data should be gathered subsequently.]

E7.2. If the validity sample is made up of records accumulated haphazardly or voluntarily submitted by test users, this fact should be stated in the manual or research report, and the test user should be warned that the group is not a systematic or random sample of any specifiable population. Probable selective factors and their presumed influence on the test variable should be stated. Essential

[Comment: While it is entirely appropriate to include in the manual such phrases as "the author and publisher of this test would welcome additional data derived from its use," it is difficult to judge the quality and representativeness of most of the resulting reports.]

E7.3. In collecting data for a validity study, the person who interprets the test results should have only that information about the examinees that is ordinarily expected to be available in practical use of the test, or he should be sufficiently trained and disciplined disregard information ordinarily not available to him. If there is any possible contamination associated with prior favorable or unfavorable knowledge about the examinees, the manual should discuss its effect on the outcome of the study. Very Desirable

E7.4. The time elapsing between the test administration and the collection of criterion data should be reported in the manual. If the criterion data are collected over a period of time, beginning and ending dates should be included. Essential

E7.4.1. Validation reports should be clearly dated, with the time interval given during which the data were collected. Essential

[Comment: Validity may deteriorate over time; in employment testing, for example, changes in jobs, work aids, and in the ability levels of applicant populations tend to change the circumstances in which validity information is developed.]

E7.4.2. In general, a test user should be cautious in making long-term predictions. Essential

[Comment: Short-term predictions are much more likely to be valid than are long-term predictions because they are less subject to influences other than the characteristics measured.]

E7.4.3. If a test is recommended for long-term predictions, but comparisons with concurrent criteria only are presented, the manual should emphasize that the validity of long-term predictions is undetermined. Essential

E7.4.4. The amount and kind of any experience or training received by the subjects between the time of testing and the time of criterion measurement should be stated. Very Desirable

E7.4.5. When validity for predicting grades in a course is reported, reasonably clear information should be provided regarding the types of performance required in the course, the nature of the instructional method, and the way in which performance is measured. If the test was administered after the course was started, this fact should be made clear. Very Desirable

E8. Any statistical analysis of criterion-related validity should be reported in the manual in a form that enables the reader to determine how much confidence is to be placed in judgments or predictions regarding the individual. Essential

E8.1. A report of criterion-related validity should give full information about the statistical analysis and should ordinarily include, in addition to such basic descriptive statistics as means and standard deviations, one or more of the following: (a) one or more correlation coefficients of a familiar type, (b) descriptions of the efficiency with which the test separates criterion groups, (c) expectancy tables, or (d) charts that graphically illustrate the relationship between test and criterion. Essential

[Comment: Full information includes data on the reliability, the strength, and the nature of the relationship. In correlational terms, this would imply information about the statistical significance and magnitude of the correlation coefficient and about the regression equation.

Reports solely of differences between group means give inadequate information regarding validity; if variance is large, classification may be inaccurate even if means differ considerably. The strength of the relationship may be indicated by describing the amount of misclassification or of overlapping. Expectancy tables may provide information about the nature of the predictions.

In general, since manuals and research reports are often directed to test users who have limited statistical knowledge, every effort should be made to communicate validity information clearly.]

E8.1.1. Errors of prediction should be estimated and reported; a validity coefficient should be supplemented with reports of the regression slope and intercept and of the standard error of estimate. Very Desirable

[Comment: The required information could be presented in an expectancy table showing the range of possible criterion values for each of several points on the score range. The standard error of estimate at different points along the score range is often helpful.

For a dichotomous criterion, this objective might be achieved by indicating the proportion of hits, misses, and false inclusions at various cutting scores.]

E8.1.2. For some users, analysis of test variance according to the following sources is appropriate: variance relevant to the criterion, variance explained as form-to-form or trial-to-trial inconsistency, and a reliable but irrelevant remainder. Very Desirable

[Comment: Such an analysis is more complete and less subject to misinterpretation than a correlation coefficient, including even a "corrected" validity coefficient, or a comparison of group means.]

E8.1.3. The method of statistical analysis should be chosen with due consideration of the characteristics of the data and of the assumptions of the method. Essential

[Comment: Data may often depart from the assumed characteristics with little ill effect. Some violation of assumptions may, however, be seriously misleading. For example, the use of predictions based on the assumption of a normal bivariate correlation surface may seriously overestimate the mean performance of high-scoring candidates if the data are markedly heteroscedastic (as in triangular scatter distributions). In such cases, a method of analysis not based on assumptions about the bivariate distribution would present a more accurate statement of validity.]

E8.2. If validity coefficients are corrected for errors of measurement *in the criterion*, the computation of the reliability coefficient of the criterion should be explained, and both corrected and uncorrected coefficients should be reported. Essential

[Comment: Coefficients corrected for errors of measurement in the *test* are not estimates of the criterion-related validity for the existing test and should not be reported. Corrections for attenuation are very much open to misinterpretation, especially if based on obtained correlation coefficients that are very low or from a small or otherwise inappropriate sample; if misinterpreted, they give an unjustifiably favorable impression of the validity of the test scores. The hazard is illustrated in the manual for an adjustment inventory. The author reported correlation coefficients between inventory scores and criterion ratings; also reported were estimated coefficients between "true" inventory and criterion scores. He then commented that the augmented correlation coefficients "are as high as those often secured between college aptitude tests and college grades." The

comparison is improper, in part, because the test author compared augmented coefficients with uncorrected coefficients for ability tests.]

E8.2.1. Where correlation coefficients are corrected for attenuation or restricted range, full information relevant to the correction should be presented. If such corrections are made, significance tests should be made with the uncorrected correlation coefficients. Essential

[Comment: Corrections should be applied only to obtained coefficients. It is ordinarily unwise to make sequential corrections, as in applying a correction for attenuation to a coefficient already corrected for restriction of range. Chains of corrections may be useful in considering possible further research, but their results should not be seriously reported as estimates of population correlation coefficients.]

E8.3. If validity is demonstrated by comparing groups that differ on the criterion, the manual should report whether and by how much the groups differ on other available variables that are relevant. Very Desirable

[Comment: Since groups that differ on a criterion may also differ in other respects, the test may be discriminating on a quality other than that intended. Types of mental disorders, for instance, are associated with age, education, and length of time in the hospital. Confounding of this sort should be taken into account when the usefulness of a test for diagnosis is appraised.]

E8.3.1. If a test is suggested for the differential diagnosis of patients, the manual should include evidence of the test's ability to place individuals in diagnostic groups rather than merely to separate diagnosed abnormal cases from the normal population. Essential

[Comment: When a test is recommended for the purpose of assigning patients to discrete categories, such statistics as contingency coefficients, phi coefficients, or discriminant functions should be supplemented by a table of misclassification rates giving, for example, the proportion of patients falsely included in a category or falsely excluded from it. Such proportions should be compared with base rates, that is, the proportions of correct classifications made possible by a mere knowledge of the sizes of the categories.]

E8.3.2. If validity is demonstrated by comparing groups that differ on the criterion (e.g., where one group is identified as a high-performance group and another as a low-performance group), all cases should be assigned to one or the other of the groups. Very Desirable

[Comment: The most reliable statistics are obtained if all cases are used; validity coefficients derived from extreme groups may be misleading. In some situations, analyses using extreme groups may be useful for identifying predictors, but generally the validity reported for any given predictor should be based on all cases. If the use of extreme groups is deemed necessary or appropriate to a particular study, appropriate estimates of correlation should be used. The typical product-moment and biserial estimates are *not* appropriate in this situation.]

E8.4. When information other than the test scores is known to have an appreciable degree of criterion-related validity and is ordinarily available to the prospective test user, the user should consider both the validity of the other information and the resulting multiple correlation when the new test information is combined with it. Essential

[Comment: Whether a test should be used for prediction and classification when other information is readily available sometimes depends not on the validity of the test but on its "incremental validity," that is, what it adds to the soundness of the judgment that would otherwise be made.

For a questionnaire intended to predict marital success, delinquency, and similar behavioral variables, the investigator should find out how much the questionnaire enhances prediction over that provided by base rates developed from demographic variables such as socioeconomic status.]

E8.5. Where more than one test is to be used, validity information should report the validity of the combination actually used. Where composite scores are developed, the basis for weighting (e.g., multiple regression equations) should be given. Essential

[Comment: In one organization, a composite was developed and validated by multiple regression in which the optimal weighting of one test was negative. Nevertheless, the organization added unweighted scores to form a different composite for use in making decisions. The multiple correlation coefficient did not, therefore, describe the validity of the test battery as it was actually used. Where a given method of combination is to be used, that method should be validated.

When multiple regression is used and one predictor in a battery is evaluated, the beta weight is a better index of its contribution to the validity of the test in that combination than is its original validity coefficient.]

E9. A test user should investigate the possibility of bias in tests or in test items. Wherever possible, there should be an investigation of possible differences in criterion-related validity for ethnic, sex, or other subsamples that can be identified when the test is given. The manual or research report should give the results for each subsample separately or report that no differences were found. Essential

[Comment: For many uses, regulations published pursuant to civil rights legislation require that validity studies be performed separately on samples differing in national origin, race, sex, or religious affiliation, when technically feasible.

The concept of fairness may involve other sources of inappropriate discrimination. For example, placing a hand-dexterity test on a low table may unfairly bias the test against tall people. The test user should try to identify potentially unfair influences on test scores in his situation. Variables which may contribute inappropriate variance may be used for subgrouping in investigation of fairness.

However, caution must be exercised in evaluating the possibility of bias. A simple difference in group means does *not* by itself identify an unfair test, although it should stimulate research to explore the question of fairness. Evidence of differential validity is developed by comparing, for example, correlation coefficients, regression equations, and means and variances for each variable.

The proper statistical test for such a difference is, for any parameter, the test of the hypothesis of no true difference between the groups, for example, a test of no difference between correlation coefficients, slopes, or intercepts. Some investigators have attempted to examine such differences by comparing in each subgroup independently the validity statistic (e.g., the correlation coefficient) to a postulated true value of zero. This is not a proper procedure; it does not answer the question at issue of *differences* in the characteristics of validity. It is impossible to demonstrate such differences by showing that one correlation coefficient, for example, is significantly different from zero while the other is not.

Users should routinely investigate differences in validity when it is technically feasible to do so, that is, when N s are sufficient for reliable comparisons and when criteria are reasonably valid in each group. Users should be aware, however, that a too-hasty acceptance of bias or of differential validity, if used in decision making, may be as likely to produce unfair test use as is failure to consider the possibility.

For example, to avoid unfairness in test use for blacks, an employer may investigate the possibility of differential validity and find not only differences in means between black and white applicants but also differences in intercepts of the regression. Some definitions of fairness require that predictions for applicants in either group should be based on the regression line developed for his own group. If the differences in intercepts are statistical artifacts (due, for example, to unreliability), the result might be considered unfair to blacks (if they have the lower regression line) since their performance might be systematically under predicted. The effect can, of course, work both ways depending on the direction of differences in regression.

It is important to recognize that there are different definitions of fairness, and whether a given procedure is or is not fair may depend upon the definition accepted. Moreover, there are statistical and psychometric uncertainties about some of the sources of apparent differences in validity or regression. Unless a difference is observed on samples of substantial size, and unless there is a reasonably sound psychological or sociological theory upon which to explain an observed difference, the difference should be viewed with caution.

Bias is not necessarily detected by criterion-related validity alone; cf. E12.12).

E10. When a scoring key, the selection of items, or the weighting of tests is based on one sample, the manual should report validity coefficients based on data obtained from one or more independent cross-validation samples. Validity statements should not be based on the original sample. Essential

E10.1. If the user recommends certain regression weights for combining scores on a test or for combining the test with other variables, the statement of the validity of the composite should be based on a crossvalidation sample. Essential

[Comment: Cross-validation is particularly necessary when the number of predictors entering the study (not the final equation) is greater than 4 or 5 and when the sample size is less than 200.]

E10.1.1. When the scoring of tests in a battery is based on regression coefficients, negative scoring weights should be used only if they have been verified by cross-validation in large samples and if their use will not be invalid (and thus unfair) to one or more subgroups in the population to be tested. Essential

E10.2. If it is proposed that decisions be based on a complex nonlinear combination of scores, it should be shown that this combination has greater validity than a simpler linear combination, that the equation can be logically explained, and that the procedures for combining scores have been cross validated. Essential

[Comment: The use of "moderator variables," for example, is to be recommended only where a moderator is shown to produce a clear improvement in validity in a cross-validation sample. Similarly, when it is proposed that some pattern of scores (e.g., high standing in scores on both Variables 2 and 5) is an indicator of success, it is necessary to show that the proportion of successful persons in the group so identified is higher than would be expected from the regression of frequency of success on a linear combination of Variables 2 and 5.]

E11. To the extent feasible, a test user who intends to continue employing a test over a long period of time should develop procedures for gathering data for continued research. Desirable

[Comment: Validity data may become obsolete. The relationship between test performance and criterion performance may be influenced by many factors, such as changes in populations, recruiting sources, the economy, organizational characteristics, processes, or tasks. Moreover, validity studies are often based on relatively few cases. A plan for the systematic collection of further data after the test has been placed into operational use may be useful both for the development of a more reliable data base and for information on changes in the trends of relationships over time.

Operational use may, however, result in severe restriction of range. Continuing research may be less necessary if the original data are based on a relatively large sample, if the bases for generalizing validity are well established, and if evidence shows a relatively slight rate of change in variables likely to limit the generizability of validity information. When these favorable conditions do not exist, it may be possible to plan for small replications from time to time rather than for a continuous program of research.]

Content Validity

E12. If test performance is to be interpreted as a representative sample of performance in a universe of situations, the test manual should give a clear definition of the universe represented and describe the procedures followed in the sampling from it. Essential

[Comment: The definition of the universe of tasks represented by the test scores should include the identification of that part of the content universe represented by each item. The definition should be operational rather than theoretical, containing specifications regarding classes of stimuli, tasks to be performed and observations to be scored. The definition should not involve assumptions regarding the psychological processes employed since these would be matters of construct rather than of content validity.]

E12.1. When experts have been asked to judge whether items are an appropriate sample of a universe or are correctly scored, the manual should describe the relevant professional experience and qualification of the experts and the directions under which they made their judgments. Very Desirable

E12.1.1. When items are selected by experts, the extent of agreement among judges should be reported. Desirable

E12.1.2. Test content should be examined for possible bias. Essential

[Comment: Bias may exist where items do not represent comparable tasks and therefore do not sample a common performance domain for the various subgroups (cf. B1.3). One may investigate such bias in terms of carefully developed expert judgments; studies of the attitudes or interpretations of items in different subgroups might also present useful information (although care must be taken to assure that the investigation is clearly directed to an analysis of content in relation to an adequately defined performance domain). The judgment of bias may itself be biased; the principle here is that, when it is possible, such judgments should be supported by data.]

E12.2. In achievement tests of educational outcomes, the manual should report the classification system used for selecting items. Desirable

E12.2.1. When an achievement test has been prepared according to a two-way content-by-process outline, that outline should be presented in the manual, with a list of the items identified with each cell of the outline. Very Desirable

E12.3. Any statement in the manual of the relation of items to a course of study (or other source of content) should mention the date when the course of study was prepared. Essential

[Comment: In achievement testing, it is frequently the practice to identify significant topics for items by a careful sampling from textbooks. Textbooks and courses of study change, however, and the test that was once an excellent sample becomes out of date. The manual might therefore report such information as the range and median of copyright dates of the textbooks examined, or the date at which the experts judged the items to be representative.

One checklist concerns problems common to students. The manual for this checklist properly reports the date when the list was assembled. From time to time, it will be necessary to determine whether student problems have changed and, if so, to change the test accordingly.

It should be recognized that this standard implies that definitions of a content universe are subject to change as jobs, society, or curricula change.]

E12.4. When a test is represented as having content validity for a job or class of jobs, the evidence of validity should include a complete description of job duties, including relative frequency, importance, and skill level of such duties. Essential

Construct Validity

E13. If the author proposes to interpret scores on a test as measuring a theoretical variable (ability, trait, or attitude), his proposed interpretation should be fully stated. His theoretical construct should be distinguished from interpretations arising on the basis of other theories. Essential

[Comment: For example, if a test is intended to measure the construct of anxiety, the test author should distinguish his formulation of the construct from other possible meanings of the term and should relate his concept to measures of anxiety discussed in the literature.

The description of a construct may be as simple as the identification of "creativity" with "making many original contributions." Even this definition provides some basis for judging whether various pieces of empirical evidence support the proposed interpretation. Ordinarily, however, the test author will have a more elaborate conception. He may wish to rule out such originality as derives only from a large and varied store of information. He may propose explicitly to identify the creative person as one who produces numerous ideas, whether of high or low quality. He may propose to distinguish the ability to criticize ideas from the ability to be "creative." He may go on to hypothesize that the person who shows originality in identifying or describing pictures will also have unconventional preferences in food and clothing. All such characterizations or hypotheses are part of the author's concept of "what the test measures" and are needed in designing and in drawing conclusions from empirical investigations of the psychological interpretation of the construct.]

E13.1. The manual should indicate the extent to which the proposed interpretation has been substantiated and should summarize investigations of the hypotheses derived from the theory. Essential

E13.1.1. Each study investigating a theoretical inference regarding the test should be summarized in a way that covers both the operational procedures of the study and the implications of the results for the theory. Very Desirable

E13.1.2. The manual should report correlations between the test and other relevant tests for which interpretations are relatively clear. Very Desirable

E13.2. The manual should report evidence about the extent to which

constructs other than those proposed by the author account for variance in scores on the test. Very Desirable

[Comment: Although it is unreasonable to require a test author to anticipate or to include every counterinterpretation in a test manual, he ought to present data relevant to those counterhypotheses most likely to account for variance in the test scores.]

E13.2.1. The manual for any specialized test or inventory used in educational selection and guidance should report the correlation of scores derived from it with well-established measures of verbal and quantitative ability in an appropriately representative population. Very Desirable

[Comment: Verbal and quantitative abilities are specified here because their importance in educational performance is recognized, because they often account for much of total test variance, and because numerous tests of these abilities are already available. To be of practical value, a new test designed to measure other constructs (e.g.,spatial abilities) must not closely duplicate the measurement of verbal and quantitative ability.]

E13.2.2. If a test has been included in factorial studies that indicate the proportion of the test variance attributable to widely known reference factors, such information should be presented in the manual. Desirable

E13.2.3. For inventories such as personality, interest, or attitude measures, evidence should be presented of the extent to which scores are susceptible to an attempt by the examinee to present a socially desirable, conforming, or false picture of himself, or to which the scores may reflect other response sets or styles. Such response patterns should be studied for identifiable subgroups rather than for a more general sample. Very Desirable

[Comment: Correlational or experimental studies might be reported. Appropriate evidence of acquiescence might, for example, be the proportion of the total test variance in the number of yes responses to the test, or by the correlation of the test scores with one or more independent measures of the acquiescence tendency, or by experimental procedures designed to induce acquiescence.]

E13.2.4. If a test given with a time limit is to be interpreted as measuring a hypothetical psychological attribute not specifically related to speed, evidence should be presented in the manual concerning the effect of speed on the test scores and on their correlation with other variables. Essential

[Comment: The most complete evidence of the effect of speed would be the comparison of scores on one form, using the usual time limit, with scores on another form having unlimited time. The correlation of scores at the end of the usual time with scores obtained with extra time on the same trial is of limited meaning because the two scores are not independent. Less complete evidence would consist of data on the percentage of examinees who attempt the last item or some item very near the end of the test. If the percentage is below 90, a more penetrating study is needed to show that individual differences on the test do not reflect speed to any great extent.]

E13.2.5. Where differences in test-taking strategies that might influence the interpretation of scores are associated with identifiable subgroup characteristics, this information should be clearly presented or its absence clearly noted. Very Desirable

E13.2.6. Where a low correlation or small difference between groups is advanced as evidence *against* some counterinterpretation, the manual should report the confidence interval for the parameter. The manual should also correct for or discuss any errors of measurement that may have lowered the apparent relationship. Desirable

F. Reliability and
Measurement Error

Reliability refers to the degree to which the results of testing are attributable to systematic sources of variance. Classical methods of estimating reliability coefficients call for correlating at least two sets of similar measurements.

One method of obtaining the two sets of measurements is by retesting with the identical test. Aside from practical limitations, theoretically, retesting is not ordinarily a desirable method of estimating reliability because the examinee may remember his or her responses to items from one testing to the next. Hence, memory becomes a systematic source of variance and the correlation of the two sets of scores may be higher than the correlation of two sets of scores based on two different but parallel sets of items drawn from the population of items in the same way.

If we want to eliminate memory as a systematic source of variance and to include the effects of item sampling and response variation over time as sources of variance, we may use two sets of items developed or selected according to the same specifications. These are called parallel forms of the test.

If the effect of content sampling *alone* is sought without the effects of memory or response variability over time, or if it is not practical to administer two parallel forms with separate time limits, reliability can be estimated from a single administration of an unspeeded test. The test may be divided into two sets of items of equal, or approximately equal, length that are judged by competent authorities to sample as nearly as possible the same functions. Any items based on the same source of data (such as a reading passage) must be assigned to the same set. Then the correlation between scores on the two parallel halves is a matched-half coefficient from which an estimate of the parallel-forms reliability coefficient for the total test may be obtained by a procedure that does not assume that the numbers of items or the variances of the two sets are exactly equal.

Estimates of reliability from a single administration may also be obtained by analysis-of-variance procedures. Such estimates will be spuriously high if the test is speeded or if the items are not independent of each other. On the other hand, for unspeeded tests, such estimates will tend to be lower than matched-half coefficients because they constitute, given certain assumptions, the mean of coefficients obtained by correlating scores on all possible pairs of halves of the test.

From the preceding discussion, it is clear that *different methods of estimating reliability take account of different sources of error*. Thus, from one testing to the other, the result is affected not only by random response variability and changes in subjects over time but also by differences in administration (especially if different persons administer the test on the two occasions). Reliability coefficients based on a single administration of a test exclude response variability over time; these effects on scores do not appear as errors of measurement. Hence, "reliability coefficient" is a generic term. It can be based on various types of evidence; each type of evidence suggests a different meaning. It is essential that any method used to estimate reliability be clearly described.

The estimation of clearly labeled components of score variance is the most informative outcome of a reliability study, both for the test developer wishing to improve the reliability of his instrument and for the user desiring to interpret test scores with maximum understanding. The analysis of score variance calls for the use of an appropriate experimental design. There are many different multivariate designs that can be used in reliability studies; the choice of design for studying a particular test is determined by its intended interpretation and by practical limitations.

It is recommended that test authors describe the meanings of any coefficients they report as accurately and precisely as possible. It is informative to say, for example, "This coefficient indicates the stability of measurement of equivalent scores based on parallel forms of the test administered 7 days apart, without intervening practice or instruction." Although lengthy, such a description is reasonably free from ambiguity.

Reliability coefficients have limited practical value for test users. The standard error of measurement ordinarily is more useful; it has great stability across populations since it is relatively independent of range of talent, and it may be used to identify limits that have a defined probability of including the true score. Test users may use reliability coefficients in comparing tests, but they use standard errors of measurement in interpreting test scores. Information in a test manual about a standard error of measurement may often be more important than information about a reliability coefficient.

General Principles

F1. The test manual or research report should present evidence of reliability, including estimates of the standard error of measurement, that permits the reader to judge whether scores are sufficiently dependable for the intended uses of the test. If any of the necessary evidence has not been collected, the absence of such information should be noted. Essential

[Comment: It is most helpful to the user when several types of reliability estimates are reported. Reports of standard errors of measurement in different groups are also helpful.]

F1.1. The test manual should furnish, insofar as feasible, a quantitative analysis of the total inconsistency of measurement into its major identifiable components; namely, inconsistency in responses of the subject; inconsistency or hetereogeneity within the sample of test content (such as the stimulus items, questions, and situations); inconsistencies in administration of the test; inconsistency among scorers, raters, or units of apparatus; and mechanical errors of scoring. Desirable

[Comment: In general, the desired analysis will not be feasible unless scores are expressed in quantitative, as distinguished from categorical or nonparametric, terms and the design of data collection includes the necessary controls.

With group tests of school achievement, the principal sources of error to be evaluated usually include: (a) inconsistency of test content; (b) inconsistencies in test administration; and (c) inconsistency in responses of the examinee over time, that is, instability. The collection of data should be designed to permit evaluation of these three factors. Fluctuation or inconsistency in the responses of the subject may be an important variable by itself; it is often a major source of random error to be evaluated. Inconsistency among scorers or raters should also be evaluated.]

F1.2. Standard errors of measurement and reliability coefficients should be provided for every score, subscore, or combination of scores (such as a sum, difference, or quotient) that is recommended by the test manual (either explicitly or implicitly) for other than merely tentative or pilot use. Essential

F1.3. For instruments that yield a profile having a low reliability of differences between scores, the manual should explicitly caution the user against interpretation of such differences, except as a source of tentative information requiring external verification. Essential

F1.4. The manual should state the minimum difference between two scores ordinarily required for statistical significance at a designated level. Very Desirable

[Comment: A nomograph or table for determining the significance of any given score difference would be a very useful addition to a test manual. "Change" or "growth" scores require careful attention to Standards F1.3 and F1.4.]

F2. **The procedures and samples used to determine reliability coefficients or standard errors of measurement should be described sufficiently to permit a user to judge the applicability of the data reported to the individuals or groups with which he is concerned.** Essential

[Comment: The mean and variance of the sample and information about its composition should be provided. Reliability data should be obtained from "natural" groups such as examinees of a single age or grade level. Estimates of the reliability of a test to be used in selecting employees should be based on scores of applicants for positions rather than scores obtained by testing college students or workers already employed.

If a test claims to be appropriate for groups from the fourth grade through graduate school, the manual should provide reliability data for each grade or age level.]

F2.1. Any identifying characteristics of the sample that may be related to consistency of performance on the test should be described in the test manual. Essential

[Comment: Demographic information, such as distributions of the subjects with respect to age, sex, socioeconomic level, intellectual level, locale, employment status or history, and minority group membership should be given in the test manual. For standardized tests, the samples used to compute reliability coefficients and standard errors of measurement should be drawn at random from the norms groups.]

F2.2. If reliability coefficients are corrected for restriction of range, both the uncorrected and the corrected coefficients should be reported in the test manual together with the standard deviations of the group actually tested and of the group to which the corrected coefficients are applicable. Essential

[Comment: When variances differ and there seem to be other justifications for such a correction, the superiority of the standard error of measurement should be noted; it is largely unaffected by differences in variance.]

F2.3. When a test is recommended or ordinarily employed in homogeneous subsamples, the reliability and standard error of measurement should be independently investigated within each subsample and reported in the test manual. Essential

[Comment: The mechanical reasoning section of a well-known aptitude test yields scores that have significantly different reliability coefficients for boys and for girls. The manual reports the reliability coefficients for each sex in each grade.]

F2.3.1. At least one estimate of the standard error of measurement should be provided in the manual for every group for which reliability data are given. Essential

[Comment: When it is specifically recommended that scores be transformed to a particular metric, the standard errors should be presented in that metric.]

F2.3.2. The test manual should report the standard errors of measurement at different score levels. Desirable

[Comment: The manual for one test of college aptitude reports standard errors of measurement for three score levels: the mean, one standard deviation above the mean, and one standard deviation below the mean. Since more important changes in the standard error of measurement are associated with extreme scores, it might be better to use more widely separated score levels if the number of cases available justifies this action.

F2.4. Item statistics (such as difficulty or discrimination indices, etc.) should be presented in at least summary form in a test manual. Desirable

F3. Reports of reliability studies should ordinarily be expressed in the test manual in terms of variances of error components, standard errors of measurement, or product-moment reliability coefficients. Unfamiliar expressions of data should be clearly described, with references to their development. Essential

[Comment: Test authors and publishers should avoid unconventional statistics unless conventional statistics are inappropriate. If unusual statistical analyses are presented, explanations should minimize the likelihood of misinterpretation.]

Comparability of Forms

F4. If two or more forms of a test are published for use with the same examinees, information on means, variances, and characteristics of items in the forms should be reported in the test manual along with the coefficients of correlation among their scores. If necessary evidence is not provided, the test manual should warn the reader against assuming equivalence of scores. Essential

[Comment: Information to be examined would include a summary of item statistics for each form, such as a frequency distribution of item difficulties and of indices of item discrimination. Content analyses of each of the forms should be presented. Thus, both frequency distributions of item statistics and a tabulation of items by categories of subject-matter content and of behavioral or instructional objectives should be furnished.

The forms should represent different samples of items within each category of content. Insofar as one's concern is for error arising from sampling a content universe, the forms to be compared should have been developed from a common universe according to an appropriate plan. An artificially close similarity between forms will result from item-by-item matching or by creating a second form merely by rephrasing items on a first form. A reliability coefficient based on forms created in this way will be spuriously high because it does not properly take into account sampling error in drawing items from the universe of items.]

Internal Consistency

F5. Evidence of internal consistency should be reported for any unspeeded test. Very Desirable

[Comment: Internal consistency is important if items are viewed as a sample from a relatively homogeneous universe, as in a test of addition with integers, a test of general high school vocabulary, or a test presumed to measure introversion. Nevertheless, estimates of internal consistency should not be regarded as a substitute for other measures.]

F5.1. Estimates of internal consistency should be determined by matched-half or random-half methods or by analysis or variance procedures, if these can properly be used with the data. Any additional measure of internal consistency that the author wishes to report should be carefully explained in the test manual. Very Desirable

[Comment: Matched-half coefficients reflect expert judgment and tend to be higher in value than random-half coefficients. Analysis of variance procedures tend to yield lower values than matched-half procedures. In unusual circumstances, special coefficients may provide useful information; if used, such coefficients

should be described so the reader will be able to understand them in relation to more conventional estimates.]

F5.2. Internal reliability estimates should not be obtained for highly speeded tests. Essential

F5.3. When a test consists of separately scored parts or sections, the correlation between the parts or sections should be reported in the test manual along with relevant reliability estimates, relevant means, and relevant standard deviations. Very Desirable

F5.3.1. If a test manual reports the correlation between a subtest and a total score, it should call attention to the fact that the coefficient is spuriously high because it is based partly on the perfect correspondence of identical errors of measurement in the subtest and in the total score. Essential

F5.4. If several questions within a test are experimentally linked so that the reaction to one question influences the reaction to another, the entire group of questions should be assigned to one of the two halves of the test when random-half or matched-half procedures are used. Very Desirable

[Comment: In a reading test, several questions about the same paragraph are ordinarily experimentally dependent. All of these questions should be placed in the same half test in using the split-half method. The fact that the test halves do not have exactly equal numbers of items need not be troublesome if an appropriate step-up procedure is used.

Comparisons Over Time

F6. The test manual should indicate to what extent test scores are stable, that is, how nearly constant the scores are likely to be if a parallel form of a test is administered after time has elapsed. The manual should also describe the effect of any such variation on the usefulness of the test. The time interval to be considered depends on the nature of the test and on what interpretation of the test scores is recommended. Essential

[Comment: For many purposes, reliability coefficients and standard errors of measurement should be based on parallel-forms procedures, with a period of perhaps 2 to 4 weeks elapsing between the administration of two parallel forms. In some situations, when test scores are obtained for changing characteristics of individuals, reliability coefficients or standard errors of measurement based on the administration of parallel forms on successive days or weeks may be desirable. A reading-readiness test used only for initial tentative assignment of first-grade pupils to instructional groups is an example. In experiments on the effects of drugs, it may be desirable to measure changes in two sets of test scores obtained before and after a time lapse of only a few minutes.

It seems reasonable to require an assessment of stability for projective techniques and other devices for assessing personality dynamics, even though it is recognized in some instances that low stability of scores over a substantial period may reflect true trait fluctuation. Clinical practice rarely presumes that the inferences from projective tests are to be applied on the very day the test is given. Realistically, one must recognize that pragmatic decisions are being made from test data which are meaningful only in terms of at least days, and usually weeks or months of therapy. If scores on a certain test are found to be highly unstable from day to day, this evidence casts doubt upon the utility of the test for most purposes, even if some fluctuation might be explained by the hypothesis of trait inconstancy. An investigator may be concerned with a psychological characteristic or educational effect which changes rapidly over a short period of time. In this instance it is important not to confuse the inconstancy of the trait with the instability of the measuring instrument.]

F6.1. Determination of the stability of scores by repeated testing should make use of parallel forms of the test to minimize recall of specific answers, especially if the time interval is short. Very desirable

F6.2. The report in a test manual of a study of consistency of scores over time should state what period of time elapsed between tests and should give the mean and standard deviation of scores at each testing as well as the correlation coefficient. Essential

F6.3. If it is reasonable to expect scores on a test to change significantly over some time interval in response to developmental or educational influences, the manual should call the test user's attention to this possibility and advise care in the use of old scores. Very Desirable

[Comment: Since some schools

administer aptitude, achievement, or interest tests only at intervals of 2 or 3 years, the manual for such tests should report correlations and changes in means and standard deviations between tests administered 1 year apart, 2 years apart, and 3 years apart. From these data the user can learn how rapidly test records become obsolete with the passage of time.]

F6.3.1. In reporting on stability, the test manual should describe relevant experience, education, or treatment intervening between administrations of the test, if known. Desirable

F6.4. Where a test is to be used to compare groups rather than individuals, standard errors and standards errors of measurement of group means and related statistics should be presented. Essential

STANDARDS FOR THE USE OF TESTS

There are many kinds of test use. As one example, test scores are used for decisions to select or to reject applicants for jobs, schools, or other opportunities. In such use, the test score is a basis for a prediction, one that is either explicit or strongly implied. The test score is used to estimate or predict a likely level of performance on some criterion variable external to the test itself.

Another use is as a prescriptive aid where different scores imply different treatments. For example, elementary school pupils may be classified according to reading ability on the basis of test scores; they may be assigned to different books or to different kinds of instruction. Job applicants may be classified as marginally employable and assigned to programs of remedial vocational training on the basis of test scores. Disturbed persons with one profile of scores may be assigned to treatments different from those for people with different profiles. Each of these examples implies a hypothesis that people with a specific set of attributes will perform a task or achieve a goal more effectively with one form of treatment than with another. The test user in an applied setting may not have the power, the resources, or the training to carry out the necessary experimental work for testing these hypotheses; he may simply accept them as part of the prevailing scientific or professional body of knowledge and use tests accordingly.

A test score may be used to certify that an individual has met some designated standard, that a person is qualified to perform certain skilled tasks, that a child is qualified for a remedial program, or that a defendant can stand trial.

The basic use of tests is descriptive or evaluative. A test score provides a description of the individual who obtained it and can help the test user to understand, analyze, or help that individual. Test scores may be used by a counselor to help a student make a vocational choice or to help a couple in marriage counseling communicate more clearly with each other. They may help a teacher work more effectively with a pupil. These are clinical, diagnostic, and individualistic uses of tests in a continuing relationship between a test user and an individual. Because the relationship is a continuing one, tentative decisions or judgments can be modified as new information is accumulated.

Test scores may constitute the dependent variable or criterion measure in an institutional research study. A program may be continued or terminated on the basis of test results; an institution may receive more or less funding because of test results; test results may be considered in organizational analysis or in making program changes. These *Standards* do not deal fully with these problems; their emphasis is more on the interpretation of scores of individuals. A companion volume is planned dealing with standards for test use in program evaluation, policy-related research, and curriculum evaluation; it will also address issues of research design and of data analysis.

The standards in the present volume are to varying degrees directed to all forms of use. As the use of tests moves along a continuum from the description of a single individual, in a situation allowing for corrections of erroneous interpretations, making decisions about large numbers of people, the test user must apply more of the standards and, perhaps, apply them more rigorously. Such decisions may profoundly influence the lives of those tested, such as decisions for employment or for attendance at college, or decisions to assign a person to one treatment or opportunity rather than to another (e.g., tracking in a school system), or decisions to continue or terminate a program or to regulate its funds. The cost of error, in money and in human suffering, may be great. A test user cannot abdicate the responsibilities described in these standards by subscribing to external testing services or test suppliers.

The standards of test use may not have to be so rigidly followed when the purpose of testing is the understanding of an individual. Sometimes such testing is less standardized than is usually recommended. For example, a school counselor may be interested in assessing the maximum performance capability of a single student. To get a full understanding of that student, he must be able to elicit new information, perhaps even through an embellishment of a standardized test, to seek the broadest possible understanding of the level of mastery and of the generalizability of the situations in which mastery can be demonstrated. Interpretation of test scores in such cases is not made in terms of norms but in terms of a counselor's analysis of what mastery of a particular skill entails (even a social skill, not likely to be measured by tests ordinarily used for content-referenced interpretations). In short, exploration of an individual case is different from standardized testing. The *user who develops test embellishments must know the difference;* that is, he must have a clear rationale for what he is doing when he departs from standard procedure, and he must be able to apply that rationale consistently and sensibly. Such individualized testing does not require less skill than does testing broadly for institutional decisions; it requires a different kind of skill (cf. I1).

The standards necessary for using tests for making decisions are not different from the standards necessary when tests are used simply for understanding, but the emphasis within a standard may be different. A test user should be familiar with the standards governing test use in general, and he should pay particular attention to those standards most nearly fitting his own specific type of application.

In doing so, he should realize that the standards are intended to apply, in principle, to *all forms* of assessment. In choosing from alternative methods of assessment, the test user should consider the differences in the ease of applying these standards.

G. Qualifications and Concerns of Users

Assessing others is an occupational activity for teachers, parents, clergymen, shopkeepers, correction officers, etc. Some people assess with remarkable skill; others are inept and have little or no training to help them. Users of educational and psychological tests in schools, places of employment, clinics, laboratories, prisons, and other places where educators and psychologists work should have had at least some formal training.

A test user, for the purposes of these standards, is one who chooses tests, interprets scores, or makes decisions based on test scores. He is not necessarily the person who administers the test following standard instructions or who does routine scoring. Within this definition, the basic user qualifications (an elementary knowledge of the literature relating to a particular test or test use) apply particularly when tests are used for decisions, and such uses require additional technical qualifications as well. A recurring phrase in discussions about testing is "the legitimate uses of a test." One cannot competently judge whether his intended use is among those that are "legitimate" (however defined) without the technical skill and knowledge necessary to evaluate the validity of various types of inferences.

G1. A test user should have a general knowledge of measurement principles and of the limitations of test interpretations. Essential

[Comment: The required level of knowledge will vary with the complexity of the evaluations to be made and the responsibility of the user. At a minimum, the user must be knowledgeable about testing principles, understand the concept of measurement error, and be able to interpret an obtained test score. He should realize that there are alternative explanations for a given score and should have a pool of knowledge from which to evaluate some of the alternatives.]

G1.1. A test user should know his own qualifications and how well they match the qualifications required for the uses of specific tests. Essential

G2. A test user should know and understand the literature relevant to the tests he uses and the testing problems with which he deals. Very Desirable

[Comment: A broad connotation is intended for this standard. The test user should have some acquaintance with the relevant findings of behavioral sciences, such as those related to the roles of heredity and environment, when using aptitude tests; some understanding of physiology is useful when one is using tests of motor skills. A very narrow interpretation of "the literature relevant to the test" is inadequate.

Unfortunately, it seems that ignorance of the literature requires that old information be rediscovered. For over 40 years, for example, it has been known that children with limited or restricted cultural exposure, such as children on canal boats or in isolated mountain communities, make low scores on intelligence tests standardized on more advantaged populations. The point has been made repeatedly in research reports and textbooks. Nevertheless, many black and Spanish-speaking children with limited cultural exposure who receive low scores on intelligence tests standardized on more advantaged groups are improperly classified as mentally retarded.]

G3. One who has the responsibility for decisions about individuals or policies that are based on test results should have an understanding of psychological or educational measurement and of validation and other test research. Essential

[Comment: A test user should have acquired the technical understanding appropriate to his responsibilities. Test users within organizations or regulatory agencies should have enough technical knowledge to be able to evaluate competently the tests and testing procedures relevant to the decisions they must make. If their technical training is limited, they should seek refresher training or work under the guidance of another test user whose training is adequate.]

G3.1. The principal test users within an organization should make every effort to be sure that all those in the organization who are charged with responsibilities related to test use and interpretation (e.g., test administrators) have received training appropriate to those responsibilities. Essential

[Comment: Serious misuse and distortion in interpretation may occur when people are not properly trained to carry out their responsibilities. The level of training needed varies with the complexity of a testing program, the level of the individual's responsibility for it, and the nature and intensity of possible adverse consequences. Test users should provide at least a basic orientation for administrators or executives who decide whether to test or

not to test, to approve or to disapprove specific assessment procedures, to appropriate funds for necessary research, or to decide how test or research results will be used in the organization. Similar knowledge is needed by compliance officers who may have a detrimental influence on testing programs because of unreasoned and unreasoning demands for interpretation of data, who might disapprove of a testing program without adequate consideration of the alternatives, or who might approve faulty and unfair uses of tests out of ignorance.]

G3.1.1. A test user should have sufficient technical knowledge to be prepared to evaluate claims made in a test manual. Very Desirable

[Comment: A test user must accept some responsibility for the choice when a test is chosen. The user must also be able to exercise some judgment concerning descriptions of intended populations that appear in a manual. If he is using the test to evaluate a remedial program for low-performing pupils in the fourth grade, it is not necessarily appropriate to select a test standardized on "children in Grades 4 through 6."]

G3.2. Anyone administering a test for decision-making purposes should be competent to administer that test or class of tests. If not qualified, he should seek the necessary training regardless of his educational attainments. Essential

[Comment: Some tests are easily administered, and a brief explanation of the instructions and of the necessity for standardization may be sufficient training for administering them. The use of other tests or assessment procedures may require more specific or unique kinds of training, for example, individually administered intellectual or personality measures or some work samples. It should be recognized that the administration and scoring of a test may not require any specific academic degree; conversely, possession of a degree is not necessarily evidence of qualifications to administer a particular test.]

G4. Test users should seek to avoid bias in test selection, administration, and interpretation; they should try to avoid even the appearance of discriminatory practice. Essential

[Comment: This is a difficult standard to apply. Sources of item or test bias are neither well understood nor easily avoided. The very definition of bias is open to question. The competent test user will accept the obligation to keep abreast of developments in the literature and, at the very least, to demonstrate a sensitivity to the problem and to the feelings of examinees.]

G5. Institutional test users should establish procedures for periodic internal review of test use. Essential

[Comment: The competent use of tests and test scores requires regular review of procedures and of concepts that may change with the advent of new knowledge. A practice that might have been considered acceptable or appropriate at an early period may be found to be either harmful or ineffective in light of subsequent findings in psychometric theory or criticisms of test use. The review should examine the soundness of procedures used in test administration, the modes of assessment, the bases for inferences drawn from test scores, and the relative quality of various validation strategies.]

H. Choice or Development of Test or Method

Standardized tests constitute one class of assessment procedures available to the user. He may also choose various kinds of ratings, personal history information, reference information, or "unobtrusive measures." He may also elect to develop his own tests. His choice depends upon what is available for assessing the characteristics of concern, ethical considerations, and his own knowledge and competency. Among standardized tests there are usually many alternatives: different dimensions to be measured, different methods of measurement, and different forms of tests. Choices should be made as deliberately and carefully as circumstances permit; test users should not use habitually the same test or method of assessment for all purposes; neither should they assess only those characteristics that are easily or conveniently assessed and fail to consider other, possibly more important, characteristics. Standards refer to the process of choice, not to the choices themselves.

H1. The choice or development of tests, test batteries, or other assessment procedures should be based on clearly formulated goals and hypotheses. Essential

[Comment: There is usually an assumption that one's goals are good, and that the method of assessment chosen will help one achieve those goals. In choosing or building a test one should be able to articulate such assumptions and values. As a general rule, the assumptions take the form of at least an implicit hypothesis: "If I come to a clearer understanding of this individual, in terms of the characteristic or set of characteristics assessed, I will be able to infer something about his vocational success, or his academic problems, or his prognosis in marriage, or whatever."

The use of a test in a decision context implies a hypothesis of the form that a designated outcome is a function of the test variable. A test user should be able to state clearly the desired outcome, the nature of the variables believed to be related to it, and the probable effectiveness of alternative methods of assessing those variables.

The purpose of administering a test should be explicit. In some school systems, it has been alleged, tests are routinely administered with no purpose other than an apparent hope that they will someday be useful. Such routine testing is unwise.]

H1.1. The test user should formulate goals clearly enough so that he can later evaluate his success in achieving them and can communicate that evaluation to other qualified persons. Very Desirable

[Comment: In a clinical or counseling situation, there is a continuing relationship with a person who has been tested. If a test user has clear purposes, later events can provide evidence of some success in achieving goals or information for changing inferences or procedures. Without a clear idea of

what is to be learned about a person, and why, there will be no clear direction in the counseling relationship.

One's purposes in developing a testing program define his criteria, and the nature of the criteria should suggest to the informed user hypotheses, that is, test variables, that might be associated with them. Such hypotheses should be reasonable. There is no clear reason, for example, to use a mechanical-aptitude test to try to predict performance in English classes. Similarly, it is not easy to see what purpose is intended when a vocabulary test is adopted for use in the selection of rolling-mill employees.

Some hypotheses are much more easily justified than others. Few people will quarrel with the suggestion that applicants who type rapidly with few errors will become preferred employees in a stenographic pool. The hypotheses that those who are likely to work with greater persistence at a routine, manipulative task can be identified by scores on a very long but easy perceptual speed and accuracy test may require a more detailed explanation of the logic and background data.]

H1.2. The test user should consider the possibility that different hypotheses may be appropriate for people from different populations. Essential

H2. A test user should consider more than one variable for assessment and the assessment of any given variable by more than one method. Essential

[Comment: For most purposes, the evaluation of a person requires description that is both broad and precise; a single assessment or assessment procedure rarely provides all relevant facets of a description.

Decisions about individuals should ordinarily be based on assessment of more than one dimension; when feasible, all major dimensions related to the outcome of the decision should be assessed and validated. This is the principle of multivariate prediction; where individual predictors have some validity and relatively low intercorrelations, the composite is usually more valid than prediction based on a single variable. It is not always possible to conduct the empirical validation study (certainly not in working with problems of individuals one at a time), but the principle can be observed.

In any case, care should be taken that assessment procedures focus on important characteristics; decisions are too often based on assessment of only those dimensions that can be conveniently measured with known validity. For example, mental retardation is often defined as both deficiency in tested intelligence and poor adaptive behavior. If both parts of this definition are accepted, then both variables should be considered in deciding whether an individual is to be classified as a mental retardate, even though it is much more difficult to measure adaptive behavior than to find an acceptable scale for testing intelligence.

Test users should also consider more than one method of assessment. Even a test yielding generally valid scores may in an individual case be susceptible to idiosyncratic errors of interpretation, and a pattern of confirming or modifying assessments may be useful. Confidence in inferences drawn from assessments may be increased by varying the sources and increasing the amount of information on which the inferences are made. In addition to tests, one might consider ratings, references, observations of actual performance, etc. Of these, a test is probably most valid. If the others add to the validity of an assessment, they should be systematically considered in statistical prediction; otherwise, they should be ignored. Frequently, however, one will not have enough confidence in test interpretations to justify overlooking other data. In particular, when using a given test with minorities, one may question the validity of test inferences for those populations and want to get as much additional information as possible before making decisions.]

H2.1. In choosing a method of assessment, a test user should consider his own degree of experience with it and also the prior experience of the test taker. Essential

[Comment: Inexperience of the test user can be alleviated by reading, practice, and training. Warm-up tests or other methods of acclimatization are advocated to alleviate the inexperience of test takers. In addition, attention should be given to the degree of interaction between test user and test taker; there may be special sources of anxiety in situations where they are of different cultural or ethnic background.]

H2.2. The choice or development of a test or test procedure, or the addition of a test or test procedure to existing assessments, should involve consideration of the relationship between the cost of the choice and the benefit expected. Very Desirable

[Comment: Both costs and benefits may involve broader considerations than the specific problem at hand. Although quantification may be difficult and even unreliable, costs and benefits to the individuals tested and to the broader society should enter into consideration.]

H3.   In choosing an existing test, a test user should relate its history of research and development to his intended use of the instrument. Essential

[Comment: A school system was faced with the necessity of reducing its faculty. Reductions in force, according to policy, were to be based on teacher competence. However, decisions were in fact based on scores on a test that had been developed to evaluate the educational backgrounds of new teachers-college graduates. Nothing about the test established its validity as a measure of classroom effectiveness, nor was any local research conducted on this point. Its choice was, therefore, inappropriate.

In a different situation, a decision had been made to use a standard achievement test to evaluate pupil progress. Upon investigation of the test's development, it was found inconsistent with the curriculum objectives of that school. Other tests were examined and an alternative test was chosen that more closely matched the curriculum content. (In some cases, closely matching curriculum content may not be advantageous since it prevents one from knowing the extent to which pupils may be deficient in skills or knowledge not deliberately specified in the local curriculum objectives.)

This standard calls for a general evaluation of the validity of the proposed use of a test. Such an evaluation includes evaluation of the procedures followed in the development of the test and of the quality and relevance of the research that has been done with it.]

H4.   In general a test user should try to choose or to develop an assessment technique in which "tester-effect" is minimized, or in which reliability of assessment across testers can be assured. Essential

[Comment: In general, the less the influence of the tester on scores, the fairer the test. The influence of the tester is obviously greater in an unstructured interview than in a structured one, and there may be more tester effect in a structured interview than in a structured personal history form. Tester effect is most likely to be minimized by standardized testing. In using tests, some organizations have turned to tape-recorded instructions in an effort to minimize further possible tester effect.]

H5.   Test scores used for selection or other administrative decisions about an individual may not be useful for individual or program evaluation and vice versa. Desirable

[Comment: The purposes of institutional testing and of evaluative testing are not always compatible. Whereas the typical evaluative use is intended to help the individual (or program), institutional decisions frequently have the apparent effect of hurting, even if the decision may have unseen long-term benefits to the individual (such as avoidance of an unnecessary failure experience). These seemingly contradictory functions may prevent effective interpretation in either instance.]

I. Administration and Scoring

A test user may delegate to someone else the actual task of administering or scoring tests, but he retains the responsibility for these activities. In particular, he has the responsibility for ascertaining the qualifications of such agents. Standards for administration apply not only to the act of testing but also to more general matters of test administration. The basic principle is standardization; when decisions are based on test scores, the decision for each individual should be based on data obtained under circumstances that are essentially alike for all.

I1. A test user is expected to follow carefully the standardized procedures described in the manual for administering a test. Essential

[Comment: It may in rare cases be necessary to modify procedures. When there is any deviation from standard practice, it should be duly noted, and interpretations of scores should not be made in terms of normative data provided in the manual. Modifications may be standardized for specific purposes. For example, modifications were necessary for testing a group of deaf mutes, but the modified procedures were applied in the same way to all children in the group.

Standardization of procedure is particularly important when decisions are based on test scores. Nevertheless, known examples of failure to follow standardized procedures are numerous. In one organization, when test supplies were depleted, mimeographed versions of uneven quality were prepared. (In addition to being a violation of copyright laws, the result was a markedly changed set of stimulus materials). One test administrator tried to relieve the monotony of the repeated verbatim instructions by giving a shorter and varied version.]

I1.1. A test user must fully understand the administrative procedures to be followed. Essential

[Comment: The test user should be fully trained to do whatever is required for competent administration of the test. The administration of many tests requires nothing more than the ability to read and understand routine instructions, that of others requires extensive supervised practice. Whatever the requirement, the test user lacking such training should seek it.]

I1.2. A test user should maintain consistent conditions for testing. Very Desirable

[Comment: Situational variables should be reasonably controlled. For example, there should be no great variation in temperature or humidity; noises and other distractions should be as nearly eliminated as possible. Interadministrator reliability should be high. In general, testing conditions should minimize variations in the testing procedure.]

I1.3. A test user should make periodic checks on material, equipment, and procedures to maintain standardization. Essential

[Comment: This standard refers, for example, to the constancy of graphics and of printing, or the accuracy of stop watches. It also seeks the elimination of bad habits that may creep into administrative procedures. It applies particularly to any testing procedures that make use of physical equipment which is subject to wear. Such equipment should be regularly examined to assure that its characteristics remain within acceptable tolerances; for example, a pegboard should be replaced if holes become enlarged or beveled through use.]

I2. The test administrator is responsible for establishing conditions, consistent with the principle of standardization, that enable each examinee to do his best. Essential

[Comment: In a negative sense, the goal of this standard is that conditions inhibiting maximum performance should be avoided. The principle can be followed in part simply by being sure that all materials—such as answer sheets, pencils, and erasers—are on hand and that precautions have been taken to avoid distractions. In a more positive sense, the administrator should be sure that the examinee understands the tasks involved in taking the test: what kinds of responses are to be made and on what answer sheets, the implications for test-taking strategy of erasures or multiple marking or guessing, and how to know whether the test has been completed.

The tester should try to create a nonhostile environment; standardized procedures are impersonal, but the test administrator must avoid being either patronizing or unresponsive to the examinees, especially when the tester and the examinee differ in race, sex, or status. A testing situation contains elements that are nonrecurring and unique to the persons tested. Although these may have negligible effects on test reliability, they may include events perceived as denigrating or questioning of the worth of the individual. A complete catalog of such events is not possible or easily described. In general, however, the social amenities of respect, politeness, and due regard for extenuating circumstances are relevant guides for insuring the dignity of persons. While it may not be demonstrated that abuse of these principles leads to poor test performance, such abuse is not likely to enhance performance.

It is often difficult to maximize the motivation of the examinees. The attempt is important; a major source of error may arise when examinees do not like or trust the test, tester, or test situation, and therefore make no special effort to do well in it.]

I2.1. Procedures manuals should be prepared for use in organizations when there is repeated testing. Very Desirable

[Comment: Just as a manual is needed for a test, a manual is needed for a testing program. Changes in personnel or lapses in memory make a record of procedures developed and followed necessary for standardization. Such a manual might indicate appropriate circumstances for testing or for referral for testing, standard sequences of tests, or guides to interpretations of test batteries in addition to instructions for administering and scoring tests tal en or adapted from individual test manuals.]

I3.   A test user is responsible for accuracy in scoring, checking, coding, or recording test results. Essential

[Comment: Any agent of the user shares this responsibility. The clerk who scores a test must understand and accept the necessity for accuracy. The test user, who may or may not do the actual scoring, nevertheless has the responsibility to be sure that procedures are established and followed for verifying accuracy. It is unfair to individuals or organizations when decisions are based on avoidable error.]

I3.1.   When test scoring equipment is used, the test user should insist on evidence of its accuracy; when feasible, he should make spot checks against hand scoring or develop some other system of quality control. Essential

[Comment: The frequency of such checks will depend on what is known of the procedures on checking within the scoring service. Commercial scoring services may be queried about their procedures if they have not already announced them; if the procedures seem well designed, such spot checks may be needed only infrequently. Some computer services, on the other hand, may be less meticulous, and some hand scoring may be required in each batch of tests scored by machine. One test user in a certification program, where machine analysis of answers not only yields individual scores but also supplies data for analysis prior to revisions, has adopted the policy of hand scoring as well as machine scoring each test. This assures the accuracy of every score used in individual decisions, and it also assures the accuracy of the computer data used in the continuing research program.]

I3.2.   When test scoring requires judgment, the test user should determine interscorer or intrascorer reliability. Very Desirable

[Comment: When the test user does his own scoring, he should make periodic comparisons of scores he has determined against scores on the same sets of responses determined by other scorers or by himself at other times.]

I4.   If specific cutting scores are to be used as a basis for decisions, a test user should have a rationale, justification, or explanation of the cutting scores adopted. Essential

[Comment: When a cutting score is adopted, the effect is to reduce scoring to a scale of only two points: pass and fail. The validity of the test scored in this way is different at different cutting scores and, in general, is different from the validity found with continuous scores.

The test user should have some justifiable reason for the adoption of a given cutting score. Many kinds of arguments might be used. In a content-referenced interpretation of a mastery test, such a score might be determined as the obtained score at which one can reject, at a preselected level of probability, the hypothesis that a predesignated confidence interval for that score includes the perfect score on the test. If interpretations are referenced against an external criterion, the cutting score might be one where there is a designated probability of achieving a specified level of success (e.g., "We do not admit students who have less than a

30 per-cent chance of graduating"). Decision theory principles can be used to find a cutting score that will maximize the discrimination between high- and low-criterion groups. One might base the cutting score simply on a distribution of scores in a "predicted-yield" situation; for example, the proportion of job applicants who accept offered employment, the number of new employees who will be needed, predictions of growth or reduction in force, and related information can be used to determined the "predicted yields" of new employees at different cutting scores. The determination of a cutting score on this basis may result in using the test in a range where it is less than maximally effective; its validity should be determined in light of its actual use.

This standard does not attempt to recommend a specific procedure for developing cutting scores where they are to be used. The intent is to recommend that test users avoid the practice of designating purely arbitrary cutting scores they can neither explain nor defend. Cutting scores adopted with reference to those used in another organization or for another purpose, or by a casual glance at normative tables, are usually unsatisfactory.]

I4.1. A validity coefficient for each criterion for which a predictor test is recommended should be provided at each one of several points on the score continuum that may be used as cutting scores. Very Desirable

I4.1.1. If examinees are to be selected on the basis of a set of scores that displays different regression lines for use in predicting the same criterion in different subgroups of an applicant population, cutting scores should be established with great caution to avoid unfairness to members of one or more of the subgroups. Essential

[Comment: There are many defensible definitions of "unfairness" in the literature, and techniques have been developed for setting cutting scores to minimize "unfairness" as defined in these ways. Test users should keep abreast of the rapidly developing literature on this topic.]

I5.   The test user shares with the test developer or distributor a responsibility for maintaining test security. Essential

[Comment: Test security is a problem whenever a lapse in security can result in changing an individual's score without making a change in his true score. For some kinds of tests a lapse of security would not be serious. If one is to be tested for achieved skill, for example, knowing and practicing the test samples might be highly recommended. In many cases, however, prior knowledge of test items or scoring procedures could destroy validity. The problem is not simply one of cheating. Security may be compromised where examinees have had much prior experience with a popular test, have been taught specific test items, or have heard a lot about the test.

I5.1. Where a probable breach of security may invalidate test inferences, the test user should employ other methods of assessment; that is, he should seek a basis for more valid inferences. Very Desirable

I5.2. All   reasonable   precautions

should be taken to safeguard test material. Essential

[Comment: The use of locked files is a minimal requirement in maintaining test security. It is important to know the recipient whenever tests are out of the filing cabinets. In a test-taking situation, examinees should be proctored. When a test is mailed out to other locations, the recipient should be known and trusted. The ubiquitous copying machine has intensified the problem of safeguarding test materials.]

I5.3. The test user should avoid basing decisions on scores obtained from insecure tests. Very Desirable

[Comment: A test may be designated insecure because it is known that unauthorized copies have gone astray. Another test might be considered insecure because it is so widely used that a test taker may have had ample opportunity to practice it in other test-taking situations previously and be able to recognize items. Some employment tests, for example, are so widely used that a job applicant may have taken them several times while applying to various employers.]

J. Interpretation of Scores

Standards in this section refer to the interpretation of a test score by the test user and to reports of interpretations. Reports may be made to the person tested, to his agent, or to other affected people: Teachers, parents, supervisors, and various administrators and executives.

J1. A test score should be interpreted as an estimate of performance under a given set of circumstances. It should not be interpreted as some absolute characteristic of the examinee or as something permanent and generalizable to all other circumstances. Essential

J1.1. A test user should consider the total context of testing in interpreting an obtained score before making any decisions (including the decision to accept the score). Essential

[Comment: The standard is that one must avoid the abdication of responsibility by relying exclusively on an obtained score. Users should, in particular, look for contaminating or irrelevant variables that may have influenced obtained scores; for example, in testing to classify school children, scores may be influenced by behavior problems, visual or hearing defects, language problems, and racial or cultural factors, as well as by ability.]

J2. Test scores should ordinarily be reported only to people who are qualified to interpret them. If scores are reported, they should be accompanied by explanations sufficient for the recipient to interpret them correctly.

[Comment: There are difficult problems associated with the question of who should have access to test scores within an organization. Certainly, curious peers should not have access to them. An individual who must make the ultimate decision to admit or to reject or to hire or to reject, or to certify or not to certify, must have the interpretation. One useful (and unanswered) question is whether such a person who lacks the training necessary for the interpretation of scores should be given that training or should be given only the interpretations of scores.]

J2.1. An individual tested (or his agent or guardian) has the right to know his score and the interpretations made. In some instances, even scores on individual items should be made known. Desirable

[Comment: Strictly speaking, this is an ethical standard rather than a standard of competent test use; it is stated here because it conflicts with technical considerations of test security. If the standard is followed, test interpretations and their foundations will be made available to those with a "need to know"; certainly, the individual whose future is affected by the decision is among those with a "need to know." The test user should take any precautions he can, when the demand for information is severe, to protect test security, but he should not do so at the expense of an individual's right to understand the bases for decisions that affect him adversely. Such understanding may be better promoted, with less threat to test security, by using qualified persons sympathetic to the individual's interests. For example, when there is a civil-rights issue, it would be most useful to have items examined by a qualified testing specialist who is known to be both concerned and knowledgeable.]

J2.2. A system of reporting test results should provide interpretations. Essential

[Comment: Although the form of a report will differ for different audiences (examinees, teachers, parents, supervisors), it should communicate the interpretation in a form that will be clear and easily understood.]

J2.2.1. Scores should ordinarily be interpreted in light of their confidence intervals rather than as specific values alone. Very Desirable

J2.3. In general, test users should avoid the use of descriptive labels (e.g., retarded) applied to individuals when interpreting test scores. Desirable

[Comment: The standard applies to the use of summary diagnoses in general. For nearly all purposes, it is better to describe behavior and to differentiate such description from inference. Summary labels tend to be inferences treated as if they were descriptions.

The use of a summary label generally connotes value judgments; unfortunately, most are words used in everyday language and therefore subject to inaccurate interpretation. A test maker may know precisely what he means when he uses the term "retarded," but he has no influence over the interpretation of the same word by a judge, teacher, parent, or child.]

J3. The test user should recognize that estimates of reliability do not indicate criterion-related validity. Essential

[Comment: Reliability is a necessary but not a sufficient condition of validity. Reliability coefficients are pertinent to validity in the negative sense that unreliable scores cannot be valid; but reliable scores are by no means *ipso facto* valid.]

J4. A test user should examine carefully the rationale and validity of computer-based interpretations of test scores. Essential

[Comment: The user of a special service has the obligation to be thoroughly familiar with the principles on which such interpretations are derived, and he should have the ability to evaluate a computer-based interpretation of test performance in light of other evidence he may have.

J5. In norm-referenced interpretations, a test user should interpret an obtained score with reference to sets of norms appropriate for the individual tested and for the intended use. Essential

[Comment: The reverse is also a standard of competent test use: The test user ordinarily should not interpret an obtained score with reference to a set of norms that is inappropriate for the individual tested or for the purposes of the testing. This is a relatively simple standard to state, but it often is difficult to apply. Contemporary social problems suggest that men and women or members of different ethnic groups should for some purposes be evaluated in terms of several norms groups. For other purposes, such as vocational counseling, students should know how they stand relative to those in or entering a relevant occupation, regardless of their ethnic background. Of course, women or members of minority groups should not be counseled to avoid non-traditional occupations (e.g., women in engineering) merely for lack of appropriate norms.

It is by no means certain that sex or race is the crucial variable in interpreting a given score. It may well be that more important variables for differential norms would be breadth of cultural exposure (or degree of cultural isolation), skill and experience in the use of standard English, interests, or similar variables which may seem to be related to sex or racial differences in test performance.]

J5.1. It is usually better to interpret scores with reference to a specified norms group in terms of percentile ranks or standard scores than to use terms like IQ or grade equivalents that may falsely imply a fully representative or national norms group. Essential

J5.2. Test users should avoid the use of terms such as IQ, IQ equivalent, or grade equivalent where other terms provide more meaningful interpretations of a score. Essential

[Comment: Such scores are objectionable for several reasons. Most important, they generally involve spurious projections of growth. They involve an interpretation which is at best awkward. (To illustrate: It is much simpler to ask, in interpreting a score, "Where does this person stand in relation to specific norm groups?" than to ask, "What group is this person's performance like the average of?" The semantic awkwardness of the latter question illustrates its psychometric awkwardness as well.) They are labels to which the general public attaches many different inappropriate meanings.

Some of these scores, such as mental age or grade equivalent scores, involve severe technical problems. For example, serious misinterpretations occur when grade levels are extrapolated beyond the range for which the test is designed. Moreover, it should be recognized that the standard error of measurement for some widely used standardized achievement tests may be equal to one grade level.

If a test user, either because of his own limitations or because of rigid institutional policies, feels that he must use such terms, he should be sure that interpretations are also given in standard scores or percentile ranks with reference to the specific norms group used in deriving them. The specific test, test form, time of testing, and nature of the test situation should be included in the statement.]

J5.3. A test user should examine differences between characteristics of a person tested and those of the population on whom the test was developed or norms developed. His responsibility includes deciding whether the differences are so great that the test should not be used for that person. Essential

J5.3.1. If no standardized approach to the desired measurement or assessment is available that is appropriate for a given individual (e.g., a child of Spanish-speaking migrant workers), the test user should employ a broad-based approach to assessment using as many methods as are available to him. Very Desirable

[Comment: The standard is to do the best one can. This may perhaps include the use of a test, even though no appropriate normative data are available, simply as a means of finding out how the individual approaches the task of the test. It might include references, extensive interviews, or perhaps some *ad hoc* situational tasks. Efforts to help solve educational or psychological problems should not be abandoned

simply because of the absence of an appropriate standardized instrument.]

J5.4. Local normative data or expectancy tables should ordinarily be developed, if possible, when administrative decisions are based on test scores. Very Desirable

[Comment: Expectancy tables may be more useful than norms. When decisions are based on test scores (with the possible exception of content-referenced interpretations), the test user has ordinarily hypothesized that some outcome on an external criterion is related to performance on the test. Decision makers will have a more useful interpretation of a test score if it is expressed in terms of an expected level of performance on the criterion than if it is expressed in terms of relative standing.]

J5.5. Ordinarily, normative interpretations of ability-test scores should not be made for scores in the chance range.

[Comment: On one reading test for elementary school students, a child who cannot read, and therefore gives truly random responses, would be most likely to obtain a grade-equivalent score, according to the norms, of 2.2; that is, second month of second grade. Quite apart from the usual difficulties with grade-equivalent scores, the example demonstrates the impropriety of trying to make a normative interpretation of a test score obtained in a chance range. One test manual for a widely used test of general mental ability has provided a useful guide to the interpretation of "range-of-chance" scores.]

J6. **Any content-referenced inter-**

pretation should clearly indicate the domain to which one can generalize. Essential

J7. The test user should consider alternative interpretations of a given score. Essential

[Comment: In a sense, a test-score interpretation implies the hypothesis that the score obtained is a function of the trait level "really" possessed. Alternative hypotheses can be suggested. The obtained score might be a function of anxiety, prior knowledge of the test, inadequate understanding of the instructions, a general sort of test wiseness, deliberate faking, or any of several other possibilities. The test user needs to consider more than the obvious interpretation and to have the skill and sensitivity necessary to develop alternative explanations and to evaluate them.]

J7.1. Where cutting scores are established as guides for decision, the test user should retain some degree of discretion over their use. Desirable

[Comment: The point bears repeating that a test user cannot abdicate the responsibility for the decision to use the test. In most circumstances, there *are* alternatives. Despite the fact that a given test may have a high predictive validity for a specific function, it may represent a trait which is not the only path to success in the predicted venture; and its validity for a given individual, tested at a particular time and under particular circumstances, may be in doubt.

This standard may *not* be taken as a license to discriminate; it is to be used sparingly in recognition that excessive subjectivity can reduce rather than enhance validity. The intent is to avoid a mechanical rigidity in using test scores of imperfect validity. See also H2.]

J7.2. A person tested should have more than one kind of opportunity to qualify for a favorable decision. Desirable

[Comment: In some situations, a candidate might be given the option to qualify on the basis of characteristics other than those measured by the test. If a person with a score so low that his best prognosis is academic failure, nevertheless succeeds in college, he may have demonstrated qualities necessary for success other than those measured by the test, and the fact might well be considered.

Again, the standard must be judiciously applied. In general, the most valid methods available should guide decisions; the subjective use of information not validated can reduce validity. When compelling information exists, however, it should not be ignored in individual cases. It should be noted that it would be unethical as well as invalid to invoke this principle in the application of particular biases of the test user.]

J7.3. A procedure for reporting test results should include checks on accuracy and make provision for retesting. Desirable

[Comment: Errors in procedures and in test scoring occur; procedures should be available for checking. Retesting is one form of checking results. There should be some limits to a retesting provision. The number of allowable retests may be limited by the number of parallel forms available. Certain types of assessments (e.g., personal–history data) are inappropriate for "retesting." Moreover, a true score is likely to be closer to the mean than is its corresponding obtained score. This fact has important implications for extremely low scores; they will tend to be increased in a retest.

In general, however, opportunities for retesting should be permitted without major obstacles. The principle is that no one should be a victim, without recourse, of an adverse decision on the basis of faulty and correctable psychological assessment. Nor should such decisions be permanent; over a period of time, individuals should have a chance for reevaluation on the basis of new learning or new experience.]

J8. **The test user should be able to interpret test performance relative to other measures.** Very Desirable

[Comment: For many uses, one should be able to interpret test scores in terms of external criteria. The necessary data may be in a test manual; manuals for some academic aptitude tests provide expectancy charts useful for such interpretations. When an assessment of performance on an external criterion is also available, and when there is a wide discrepancy between actual and predicted criterion performance, the test user should investigate possible reasons for the discrepancy. Furthermore, there should be no *a priori* assumption that either the test or the criterion is the instrument in error.]

J8.1. A test user should be able to use and interpret data regarding the statistical significance of differences between scores. Very Desirable

[Comment: A test user may observe differences in scores made by two individuals on the same test. There may be differences in the scores made by an individual on a pretest and a posttest after some intervening treatment or training. He may be interested in comparing the individual's performance on one test with the same person's performance on still another test. In such cases, the test user should know how much confidence to place in an observed score difference.]

J9. **A test user should develop procedures for systematically eliminating from data files test-score information that has, because of the lapse of time, become obsolete.** Essential

[Comment: Data should not even be available for consideration in decision making after an invalidating period of time. Scores on early achievement tests in areas where later learning or forgetting is to be expected (e.g,, an old typing-test score) are no longer likely to be valid.

Not all data are equally susceptible to obsolescence. Information of a highly subjective nature might be judged to become obsolete in a shorter time than more objective items of information. Information about young children might be judged to become obsolete in a shorter period of time than comparable kinds of information about adults.

In the case of data that have potential value for research or for survey purposes, the purging may consist of destroying the link between a person's name and the information relevant to the test rather than destroying the information itself.]

INDEX